# *The* RIVER DART

***An Illustrated Exploration of the Dart Estuary***

To Pauline

with best wishes

John Risdon

June 2004

• HALSGROVE DISCOVER SERIES ➤

# *The* RIVER DART

## *An Illustrated Exploration of the Dart Estuary*

JOHN RISDON

HALSGROVE
In association with

First published in Great Britain in 2004



**British Library Cataloguing-in-Publication Data**
A CIP record for this title is available from the British Library

ISBN 1 84114 355 3

**HALSGROVE**
Halsgrove House
Lower Moor Way
Tiverton, Devon EX16 6SS
Tel: 01884 243242
Fax: 01884 243325
email: sales@halsgrove.com
website: www.halsgrove.com

Printed and bound by D'Auria Industrie Grafiche Spa, Italy

## Contents

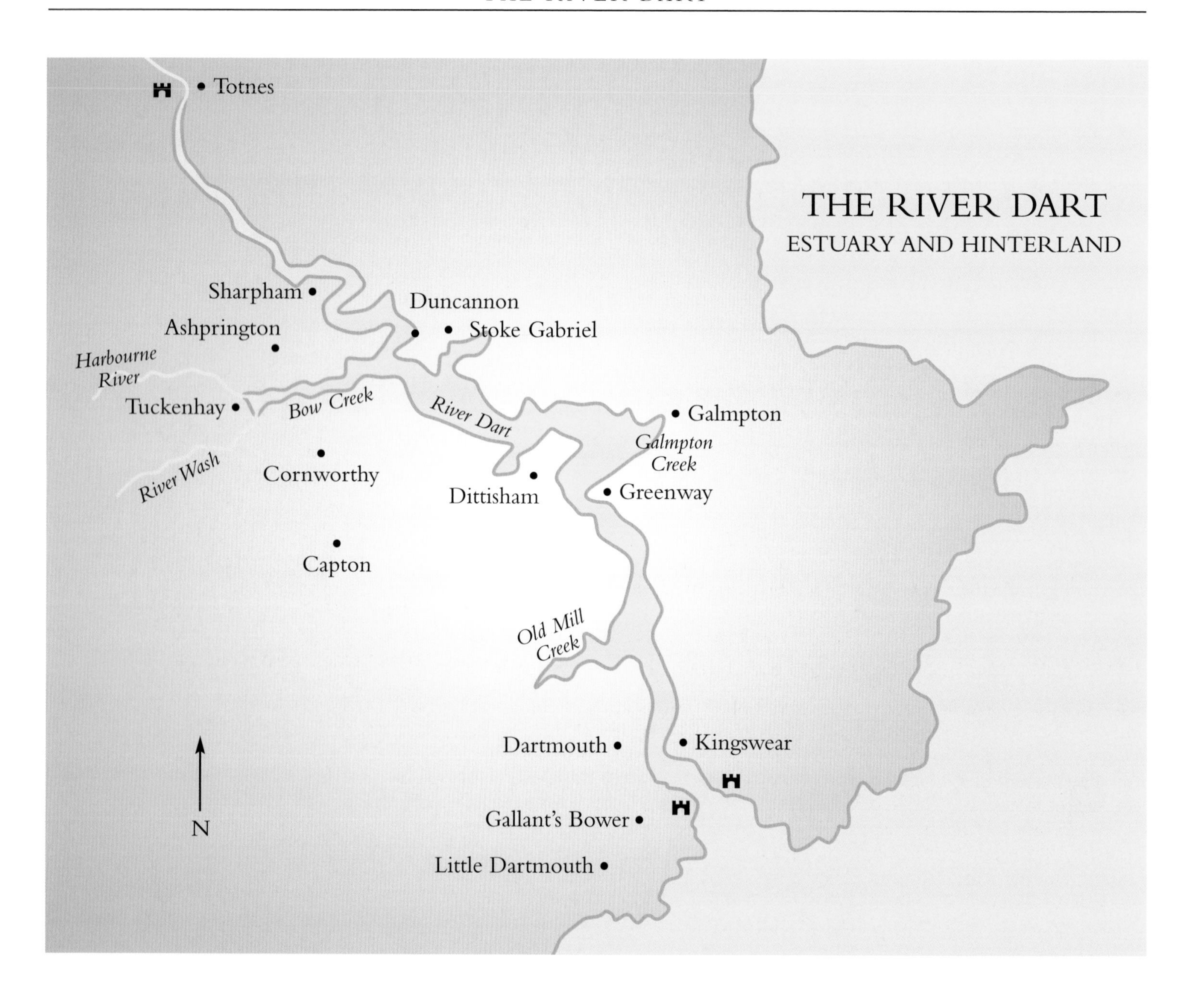
THE RIVER DART
ESTUARY AND HINTERLAND
Totnes
Sharpham
Duncannon
Ashprington
Stoke Gabriel
Harbourne River
Tuckenhay
Bow Creek
River Dart
Galmpton
Galmpton Creek
River Wash
Cornworthy
Dittisham
Greenway
Capton
Old Mill Creek
Dartmouth
Kingswear
Gallant's Bower
Little Dartmouth
N

# The Dart Estuary – Nature's Tidal Highway of South Devon

The Dart estuary forms the final eleven miles (18km) of one of Devon's best-known rivers, taking its name from the moorland from which it rises. Its estuarine course lies in the general direction south-by-south-east and its waters enter the English Channel at the northern extremity of Start Bay. The estuary provides a physical division between the communities of Torbay to the east and the rural expanse of the South Hams to the west.

*Secret doorway to a magical river.*

The river and its estuary have played a major part in the history of the region throughout the centuries. Human settlement over the past thousand years is principally evidenced in the towns of Dartmouth and Totnes, sitting comfortably at either end of the river's tidal reach. It could be said that it is by a quirk of fate that we find the estuary as it is today, but a far more defined path, influenced by the realities of geography and the vagaries of mankind, can be traced.

The following chapters and accompanying photographs are a celebration of the Dart estuary and its history. Much has changed; the shipyards and commercial wharves of the port of Dartmouth, the demise of salmon fishing, just two examples. One of the aims of this book is to provide the reader with an insight into just how the communities of the Dart estuary have evolved, and one of the best ways to achieve this is by walking through the area. Here then are thirteen selected walks through town, village and undulating Dart countryside set within some of the most superb scenery in Britain. The walks are diverse, not only in content but in accessibility, so there is something here to suit everyone, from the exertions of the Dart Trail to a gentle stroll along Dartmouth's Embankment. For those no longer able to take on the challenges of a country walk it is hoped that the words and pictures will provide the

*A moment of contemplation overlooking Old Mill Creek.*

medium for transporting the imagination and spirit on a journey along this stimulating valley.

The key to the Dart's appeal is its sheer natural beauty and diversity of topography and wildlife. Having some understanding as to how it came into being physically is an essential part of appreciating how it has developed. The Dart estuary is decidedly youthful in geological terms having only been in its present state for about the last 6000 years. The sea and the river have been the major influences in the formation of the surrounding countryside. The South Devon landscape as a whole is characterised by a series of varying ancient sea levels, planing off hilltops at specific heights and forming a plateau effect. From vantage points where a panoramic view over the countryside is possible, such as at Totnes Castle or the Beacon at Bozomzeal above Dartmouth, this phenomenon is readily apparent. This landscape was formed in recent geological times, during the past two million years and the period of the great Ice Ages. South Devon was never covered by glacial ice, but the advance and retreat of the ice to the north caused great variations in sea levels, creating the landforms we see today. The present coastline through which the Dart enters the sea graphically illustrates this incised-plateau surface, with hilltops around the 425 feet (130m) mark. Further inland an even higher ancient sea-level of 590 feet (180m) can be identified around the hilltops of Greenway and Ditttisham.

*The Port of Dartmouth from Bozomzeal. The skyline – an ancient marine plateau incised by the power of a primeval mountain torrent.*

The Ice Age comprised at least eight cold periods when glacial ice advanced south over the landscape. These were interspersed with what were known as inter-glacial, or warmer periods, when the ice retreated. During the cold periods, sea levels were lower than today and the coastline was further east than its present position. With the thaws of the warmer periods, huge amounts of water were released from the melting ice to the north and poured over the Devonian landscape on their way to the distant sea. At times, these rivers would have been similar to the great torrents of the Rockies and northern Russia today, rivers that had the energy and erosive power to cut out deep valleys such as the Dart.

Ten thousand years ago saw the end of the last period of the Ice Age. Sea levels were 100 feet (30m) lower than today and the River Dart entered the sea to the east of its present position. The length of the entire present estuary would have been devoid of any tidal influence and the freshwater course would have run along the valley floor as it tumbled towards the sea. With the melting of the ice, sea levels began to rise once more and the sea began its slow encroachment, gradually submerging the valley floor until, around 6000 years ago, much of the natural estuary had been formed, with the influence of the tide now reaching many miles inland. Even today sea levels are continuing to rise!

*The heights of Gallant's Bower (in the middle distance) rise up over the drowned depths of the Dart valley – a natural haven for generations to come.*

Otherwise known as a ria, or drowned valley, the Dart is but one of many such estuaries along the coast of Devon and Cornwall, although the facts associated with its geography and structure make it unique. At its mouth, the valley is over 500 feet in depth with 100 feet now filled with sediments and the sea. The depth of water provided relatively easy access for vessels with no sand bar to

*The lower reaches of the estuary as seen from the heights above Greenway.*

obstruct navigation as found at the mouths of the Teign and Exe. Once inside the anchorage the depth of water ranges between 16 feet (5m) and 55 feet (17m) at low water, providing adequate space for manoeuvring, whilst the surrounding heights and interlocking spurs of land sheltered vessels from both running seas and stormy blasts, from whatever direction. It was indeed a perfect natural harbour. So here began the development of the deep-sea port of Dartmouth (with Kingswear), whilst at the farthest reach of the tide, amongst the salt marsh and shallows, was the first feasible fording place This, the lowest bridging point, later became the site of the strategic and trading inland port of Totnes.

The variety of channel and intricate meanders of the estuary, which add so much to its attraction, were formed long before the inundation of the sea and were largely influenced by local geology. The oldest rocks are sedimentary slates and shales of the Devonian period laid down on an ancient sea bed between 375 and 400 million years ago. In and around the lower reaches of the river and along the shoreline they have been given the parochial name of Dartmouth Slates and Shales. Later and very much in contrast was the

*An evocative view of the upper reaches, with the town of Totnes and distant Dartmoor providing the centrepiece. Joseph Turner sketched this scene two centuries ago.*

intrusion of volcanic lavas, tuffs and sills, all very much more resistant than the softer slates and shales. The early river course followed the line of least resistance, eroding the softer sediments as at Broad Reach and Long Reach, off Galmpton and Stoke Gabriel, whilst meandering around the harder spurs of volcanic rock, such as at Sharpham and Greenway, here cutting more restricted and incised trenches into the landscape. With the coming of the sea and the passing of time sediments were laid down along the estuary floor and its associated tidal creeks. Towards the estuary mouth these deposits are considerable, providing a sedimentary layer up to 100 feet (30m) deep.

By the time of arrival of the early European traders in what is known as the Bronze Age (4000–2500BC) the warming climate had created an estuary environment rich in vegetation and wildlife. Geoffrey of Monmouth, writing in the twelfth century, mentions an earlier link of the estuary with this prehistoric time and the travels of Brutus the Trojan. We will see his legendary signature in the Brutus Stone of Totnes, possibly a reference to early trading up the estuary. Certainly a scattering of Bronze Age people were by now creating a life for themselves along the Dart, involved in both farming and fishing the

Right: *Distant Galmpton and its adjacent creek lie over Blackness Point and nearby Dittisham Mill Creek.*

Below: Leader – *a Brixham fishing smack, built by Gibbs of Galmpton in 1892, participating in the Dartmouth Regatta sail-past.*

abundant waters of the river. Flint artefacts of this era have been found on both sides of the estuary, at Churston and at Capton. Also at Brownstone, above Kingswear, the remains of a Bronze Age barrow or burial chamber have been discovered. In the Iron Age, circa 500BC, the defensive pound of Noss, high above the tidal creek, had been constructed as a gathering point for outlying communal groups during times of threat, or possibly as a social focal point. Later the Romans brought influences of civilisation, aspects of their ways often incorporated into local native groups as found in the Romano-British farmstead close by Stoke Gabriel.

With the arrival of the Saxons came the establishment of so many of our present towns and villages. Saxon Tunstal was to be the forerunner of Norman Dartmouth, with Totnes providing its own identity from the start. The villages of Dittisham, Galmpton, Stoke Gabriel, Duncannon and Tuckenhay were all also spawned during the birth of feudal England. For these communities the river provided an artery for both communication and trade, and this vital link continued until the invention of the internal combustion engine and into the twentieth century. The estuary provides relatively few individual dwellings along its banks, but for those such as Lower Kilngate and Maypool the river provided a far easier way of reaching the markets of Dartmouth or Totnes than by going overland. Also for the landed gentry of Greenway, Waddeton, Sandridge or Sharpham, the river provided direct access to the centres of population at either extremity of the estuary and thereby links to the wider world, hence their provision of private boathouses, tucked in snugly along the shoreline.

By the fourteenth century the importance of Dartmouth and Totnes as trading ports was recognised by the Crown. Also strategically, the port of Dartmouth was becoming far more significant both locally and nationally as a contributor to the nation's naval resource during the Hundred Years' War with France. However, it was the wealth being created by the communities of the Dart that was the attraction for Edward III in bequeathing 'The Waters of The Dart' to his son, the Black Prince, Duke of Cornwall, in 1338. Administered originally as the Waterbaileywick, its rights were to include – all the land covered by the water at high tide within its area, with the right to charge dues on anything that floated, moored, was beached, or anchored, as well as tolls on cargoes imported or exported. Also a right to a share in any 'wreck of the sea' and prize ships taken in war. Today the Duchy continues its right of ownership of 'the waters of the Dart', although, no doubt, its rights to prizes of war have since been amended.

For its working communities the estuary provided a means to a livelihood and survival over the centuries. For the salmon fisherman, the shipwright, the charcoal burner, the coal lumper, the quarryman and the farm labourer, the river and its boundaries were places of work. How often, one wonders, did they have time to admire the beautiful landscape and note the flight of the heron?

The latter part of the twentieth century has seen the final demise of the majority of working practices associated with the river: shipping, shipbuilding, quarrying, sand-dredging, amongst others, are all now confined to posterity. The last salmon skiff was built at Galmpton during the 1980s and a much reduced fishery struggles to survive. There is however a glimmer of hope for the resurgence in oyster farming now that the state of cleanliness in the river has been much improved.

As the clamours of the estuary's industrial past subside into history they are succeeded by a very different river environment. To a large extent three

*A crabber lies alongside the Dartmouth pontoon whilst the* Sir Malcolm Miller *prepares to set sail for New Zealand.*

words cover the present-day activity of the Dart estuary: conservation, tourism and leisure. While the term conservation in its present meaning did not exist in the lifetime of Charles Seale-Hayne it was he, together with Richard Harvey of Greenway, who was probably the first to take steps in Victorian times to protect and enhance the river landscape, protecting it from what they saw as unacceptable development. For Seale-Hayne this was the protection of the river mouth from housing development and the planting of woodland, for Harvey, it was the realignment of the Dartmouth and Torbay railway line and the removal of plans for a bridge across the estuary at Greenway.

Since those days, the National Trust has become the guardian of over 1100 acres of the Dart estuary. Since 1974, as part of Enterprise Neptune, the Trust has been gifted fifteen separate parcels of land abutting the Dart, from its mouth at Brownstone and Gallant's Bower, to, most recently, the Greenway Estate, donated in the year 2000. The status of Heritage Coast and Area of Outstanding Natural Beauty encapsulates a unique identity and recognition of the area of which the National Trust is well suited as guardian, protector, manager and interpreter. Conserving the estuary is an infinitely delicate task as it remains a living landscape containing working communities.

*A vessel of the River Link fleet off Greenway, returning to Dartmouth.*

The working vessels of today are largely passenger boats carrying cargoes of visitors, their objective to enjoy the natural splendour of the river and its associated historical sites. In comparison with the past, work is now for the relatively few, the multitudes are now those seeking relaxation and leisure, often in their numerous leisure craft of every size and shape. The shipyards have given way to marinas providing for the needs of these boat-owners, locals and visiting yachtsmen alike, and it is leisure and pleasure that now fill the financial coffers of local commerce. The Dart estuary is now seen as a sacrosanct environment by the majority of those who live, work and play within its boundaries, and any plans to build new commercial structures or housing within its environs are met with suspicion and determined resistance. The tough, hard-working, often dirty, ever-evolving Dart estuary of the first millennium has entered a period of aesthetic challenge but one that will continue to be moulded by the influences of local and national economics and world affairs, for better or for worse.

Posterity has provided us with a 'river of gold' as so often reflected under the setting sun. I trust the following chapters will add to the reader's enjoyment and appreciation of this precious landscape.

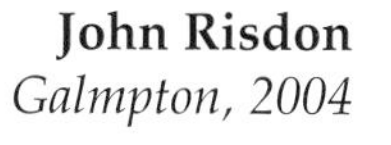

**John Risdon**
*Galmpton, 2004*

## NOTES ON USING THIS BOOK

The aim of this book is to provide the reader with an informal guide to exploring the Dart estuary and its hinterland. There are no strict routes to follow and the more adventurous can make their own discoveries. Even so the reader is invited to use this book in association with the relevant Ordnance Survey maps of the area. Start and end points for each walk are included, along with an OS map reference. These locations are often suggested with the car user in mind.

While every care has been taken to ensure that the information in the book is correct, the publisher accepts no responsibility for any inaccuracies regarding times of opening or public access. None of the walks in the book should be taxing for the healthy walker but the reader should satisfy themselves they are capable of undertaking strenuous routes. Sensible footwear and clothing appropriate to the weather conditions should be worn. Additional care needs to be taken on cliff walks, and in areas affected by tides. In rural areas follow the Country Code.

CHAPTER 1

# *Harbour Mouth – The Western Shore*

Whether leaving or entering the Dart the sheer physical presence of high hills dipping abruptly to the sea and river provide the harbour mouth with a unique identity all its own. Here we look out upon irregular and serrated cliffs slanting into the sea, a patchwork of woodland, pasture and yellow gorse, and broad horizons of ever-changing seas and skies. Here we begin our journey.

We start to the west, 394 ft (120m) above sea level and half a mile inland at what is known as Little Dartmouth, a cluster of farm buildings and cottages with an associated Regency-style farmhouse. The National Trust are now landlords of much of this coastal belt and farmland, either donated or purchased as part of Enterprise Neptune. A small car park and picnic area (SX874492) are strategically positioned at the end of the lane leading down from the Dartmouth–Stoke Fleming road, providing an ideal starting point for a circular walk taking in the mouth of the river.

*The broad sweep of Little Dartmouth farmland leads down to the open arms of the sea and the distant Mew Stone.*

Initial experiences can set the mood for the day to come and the gradual, direct descent from Little Dartmouth to the cliff-line certainly stimulates the senses. In some ways it reminds one of taking one's seat in the theatre; that walk down the aisle with all the anticipation it instils. Here the stage is set before us, a wide sweep of Start Bay framed between the Mew Stone to your left and Start Point to your right. Here, 280 ft (85m) above the sea and Warren Cove, we join the South West Way Coastal Path and turn eastwards towards the mouth of the Dart. From here, as from many such vantage points, the coastline appears to continue unbroken by the River Dart. But it is not only from the land that the river mouth has remained so well hidden, a number of sea marks have been required to assist ships' masters in finding this 'hidden doorway' of the South Hams.

*A serrated coastline viewed from Combe Point with the old coastguard cottages standing sentinel over the mouth of the river.*

The path, set back from the cliff edge, follows the indentations and undulations of the bared Dartmouth slates as they dip in mottled hues of grey, brown and blue beds into the sea below. Vegetation is sparse and windswept, the ever-present bright yellow patches of gorse, or furze as it is known locally, interspersed with clumps of rounded blackthorn in the more sheltered nooks and crannies. Prominent along this section stands Combe Point, once a coastguard lookout station. Visible below are the remnants of a more ancient coastline, rocky outcrops jutting out of the sea and providing temporary perches for the numerous seabirds, gulls and cormorants being the most common. For early mariners these rocks guarding the approaches to the river mouth were a considerable hazard, as they are today in an easterly breeze. Immediately off Warren Point are the Dancing Beggars whilst to the north of Combe Point lie Meg Rocks. The greatest danger of course comes from those rocky outcrops lurking just below the surface, one such being Homestone Ledge, marked by the red Homestone buoy which also delineates the western side of the safe passage for larger ships entering Dartmouth.

By the time the path has descended to Blackstone Point and almost to sea level we are now well-and-truly within the official bounds of Dartmouth Harbour and on the banks of the Dart. The demarcation line runs across from Combe Point to Inner Froward Point on the Eastern shore. The coastpath now heads north and climbs up around, respectively, Ladies Cove, Deadman's Cove and Sugary Cove, and for the first time we find ourselves walking under the lush foliage of the Dart valley woodlands. The path brings us down to the narrows below Dartmouth Castle where the river is now a mere 380 yds (350m) in width (it is a mile across less than a mile upriver at Combe point). With the high hills on either side, enfolding deep water beneath the keel (at least 25 ft (8m) in the main channel), mariners know a safe haven has been reached.

There can be no surprise that this bottleneck in the rivermouth provided a suitable site for human activity. It is likely that followers of Petroc, a Celtic prince of the sixth century AD created a monastic cell on this site. Its inhabitants would have attended to the spiritual needs of both locals and visiting mariners, possibly also providing a beacon to help guide craft into the safe haven. This structure was eventually developed into the church of St Petrox.

*The Church of St Petrox. A place of spiritual tranquillity in preparation for a mariner's journey into the unknown.*

Predating the Norman Conquest a document associated with nearby Little Dartmouth refers to a 'minster' on this site, and by 1192 the origins of the present church have been noted. St Petrox is one of the few remaining Celtic placenames in Devon, the majority having been superseded by Saxon names.

Habitation and use of this early chapel seem to have been spasmodic until 1438 when Bishop Lacy granted an indulgence 'for the building, maintaining and repairing of a parochial chapel with cure of St Petrox'. This building, comprising a single aisle, corresponds to the south aisle of the present church, the north aisle being added in 1641. St Petrox originally lay within the Parish of Stoke Fleming, as did the southern portion of Dartmouth, known as South Town. This chapel provided a closer place of worship for the inhabitants of South Town than the Parish church at Stoke Fleming, and they continued to maintain and support it until 1831.

The physical position of St Petrox with its intimate little churchyard, perched precariously above the rivermouth, is immensely evocative. A scene captured here by the artist Joseph Turner in 1811 epitomizes the links this little church has had with the sea over the centuries. Turner was to witness and sketch a wedding between a number of sailors and their brides. With mariners at sea for such long periods, it was customary for marriages to take place en masse and, following the wedding ceremony, Turner caught the moment of dancing and joy, with garlands of flowers bedecking the greensward adjoining the church.

*The remains of Hawley's fortalice, constructed between 1388 and 1400.*

It seems an irony that a house of God and its association with spiritual love, should sit cheek-by-jowl with a house of war, and yet that is a fact of life as far as Dartmouth is concerned. As Dartmouth developed as a trading port of importance so grew the need to protect it from its enemies. The first defensive structure was built on the hillside above the present access road to St Petrox. Today all that remains is a section of the southernmost, or upper, curtain wall. This building, constructed between 1388 and 1400, was classified as a 'fortalice'. The man largely responsible for its construction, following strict instructions from Richard II and his government, was John Hawley, and hence it was referred to as Hawley's fortalice. So great was the threat of attack from the French and Bretons at this time, resulting from a series of tit-for-tat raids across the Channel, that the king gave Dartmouth the sole rights to export Dartmoor tin in order to fund the building of the fortalice. John Hawley and his successors were the dominant family of Dartmouth during the late fourteenth and early fifteenth centuries. Their energy and ruthlessness provided much of the driving force in the successful development of late-medieval Dartmouth. Hawley combined the roles of sea captain, merchant trader and privateer and still had time to be Mayor of Dartmouth on fourteen occasions.

*Dartmouth Castle: Tudor state-of-the-art defences, constructed 1481–1491.*

During the fifteenth century the fortalice became a suitable site for the building of a Manor House for the Carews, Lords of the Manor of Stoke Fleming. To complete the defence of the rivermouth, a chain was positioned across the river between an anchorage on the rocks below the fortalice to a small fortification on the opposite shore, by the name of Gommerock. Should the harbour mouth be threatened a winch would raise the chain and any ship trying to enter would have its bottom ripped out.

It seems highly likely that news of Dartmouth's new defences reached the ears of the town's enemies, the Bretons, on whom it had a deterrent effect. During April 1404, having burnt Plymouth, a Breton force of 300 ships landed 2000 knights plus their supporting crossbowmen at Slapton, having decided a frontal attack on Dartmouth was unlikely to succeed. From Slapton they advanced along the coast to attack Dartmouth from the rear but were met above the sands of Blackpool by a local militia force from Dartmouth, including many women. This irregular force routed the Breton army, much to the surprise of King Henry IV and his Court in faraway London, and the singing of the Te Deum in Westminster Abbey was ordered by the King.

A century later, and with Henry VII now on the throne, the adversarial contest across the Channel still continued. But by now technology had introduced gunnery into the field of warfare. With it, the fortalice became outdated and therefore between 1481 and 1491 the new castle, comprising round and square towers, was constructed. It was positioned much closer to the water's edge with its original guns, aptly named murderers, positioned as close to the water level as possible. At the time of its construction Dartmouth Castle was a state-of-the-art defence, in fact the first purpose-built fortification specifically to house cannon. A second castle with cannon was also built across the river, Kingswear Castle, but more of this in Chapter 3. However, with the crossfire that these two castles could now bring to bear on any attacking ships, together with the chain, still utilized, the port of Dartmouth remained nigh impregnable from the sea.

The chain barring the harbour remained in use throughout the Spanish threat during Elizabeth I's reign and then again during the Civil War. As the years past and gunnery evolved, so the castle defences were updated and a battery, known as Lamberd's Bulwark, was created outside its walls. During each succeeding century changes were made, with the nineteenth century witnessing the positioning of five 64-pounder guns, two of which remain today, to deter yet a further, feared, French attack in the 1860s. During the Second World War two 4.7-inch guns were positioned here, adding to the firepower of the Brownstone Battery (see Chapter 3) on the Kingswear side of the estuary. Once more the principle of that medieval chain returned in the form of an anti-submarine net stretched across the river. To complete the defences a torpedo battery was situated upstream of Kingswear Castle. The low, squat building that housed the torpedo tubes, close to the water's edge and well camouflaged by the surrounding cliffs, can still be seen today from the river or the Dartmouth Castle shore.

To complete our account of historic buildings situated here at the doorway to the Dart we return to that original Celtic concept of a guiding light to welcome mariners at the end of their voyage. The cream-coloured crenellated tower standing adjacent to the entrance to the castle was originally a mid-Victorian lighthouse built in 1856 by Charles Seale-Hayne, one of Dartmouth's landed gentry who played such a crucial part in the port's Victorian development.

Dartmouth Castle is today managed by English Heritage and is open throughout the year. The interpretation of the castle and its development is superb and confirms in every way the importance of this site in Dartmouth's history.

*The earthworks associated with the Royalist redoubt situated on Gallant's Bower.*

From the castle we initially retrace our steps up past Hawley's fortalice and then on to the ascent of Gallant's Bower. The climb up to the summit at 350 ft (150m) is relatively steep but the National Trust have improved the path considerably and the rewards are impressive, to say the least. The heights of Gallant's Bower dominate the entrance to the Port of Dartmouth with views both out to sea and upriver to the town of Dartmouth and beyond. It becomes abundantly clear why the Royalists, during the Civil War, constructed a redoubt here to assist in the defence of the town below.

The town and the port's fortunes alternated with the rise and fall of King Charles' grip on his kingdom. Dartmouth, being a town of trade and merchants, originally sided for Parliament but by November 1643 had fallen to Royalist forces under Prince Maurice. However, its determination to hold out for a month, delayed Maurice's advance on Plymouth, allowing that city to prepare more readily for the forthcoming three-year siege that ended with success for the Parliamentary forces. For the next three years Dartmouth was a Royalist port but very much limited by a Parliamentary naval blockade. As the fortunes of war swung away from the king so the defences of Dartmouth were strengthened, including the construction of Gallant's Bower redoubt under the command of Sir Edward Seymour of Berry Pomeroy. Following the arrival of Fairfax at Plymouth in January 1646 and the lifting of the siege, his attention turned to taking Dartmouth which fell relatively easily, some thousand Royalists being sent home having sworn not to take up arms against Parliament again.

The summit of Gallant's Bower has in recent times been cleared of scrub and woodland and the Civil War earthworks are clear to see, in springtime immersed in a swathe of bluebell, red campion and forget-me-not. It makes a fitting spot to ponder the folly of man's inability to manage his affairs and differences without reverting to war, especially the worst of all, civil war.

Above: *The springtime view from Gallant's Bower looking out to sea.*

Left: *Dartmouth in perspective.*

Looking towards Dartmouth, and dividing us from the town, is the Week Valley with Warfleet at its confluence with the estuary. During Stuart times, Nicholas Roope, an influential merchant and shipowner, lived here. He was for Parliament and personally fought in the original defence of the town. He lost much of his property during the Royalist period of occupation, making his way to Plymouth for the three-years of the siege. Near the head of the Week Valley and where this walk comes full-circle at Little Dartmouth, lived his cousin, Amrose Roope, landowner and Royalist.

We exit Gallant's Bower through a small gate and the path takes us through woodland to join a tarmac lane leading on up to Compass Point and Compass Cottages, once accommodation for coastguard personnel and their families. This was one of the spots where boys associated with the coal bunkering service of the late nineteenth century waited to watch out for ships coming in to coal, then racing each other down to Bayards Cove in order to 'win' the right to load that ship.

The route back from here to Little Dartmouth is relatively direct and level after the exertions earlier on the route. The view of Start Bay is soon hidden by high Devonian banks, with only rare glimpses of the sea through sporadic gateways, as we follow an unmetalled lane back to the farmyard and our starting point. This brief circuit has introduced us to the magic of the Dart, its marriage with the sea and a taste of its breadth of history spanning the centuries. We now cross the river to explore the eastern shore of this hidden doorway of South Devon.

Chapter 2

# *Harbour Mouth – The Eastern Shore*

The Southernmost heights of the Kingswear/Brixham peninsula rising to 525 ft (180m) provide a magnificent setting and a fine starting point for our exploration of this eastern shore of the Dart at its entry into Start Bay. Again the National Trust are guardians of the majority of the land associated with this walk and specifically the coastline and land associated with the river-mouth. The National Trust car park (SX905510), adjacent to Coleton Farm, is accessible off the B3205 Kingswear road, initially following the signs for NT Coleton Fishacre. The car park is surrounded by farming settlements of considerable antiquity whose roots go back at least to the Bronze Age. Within a stone's throw of Brownstone farm are the remains of a Bronze Age barrow and cist (on private land), excavated in 1932 to reveal remnants of cremated bone and a green jadeite polished axehead. Neighbouring Kingston with nearby Kingswear, as their names suggest, are very likely to have been held under common ownership of the king during Saxon and Norman times.

The landscape at and around our starting point is characterised by its open and very often wind-swept features. The 297 acres of Higher Brownstone farm have been under the stewardship of the National Trust since 1981 and thus this great swathe of strategically positioned land, reaching down to the sea and the river mouth, is well protected in perpetuity.

For South Devon, the lack of tree growth is very apparent but adds to the ease of visibility in all directions as we progress along the initial stages of the route. This follows the line of the old Second World War army track down to Brownstone Battery. Evidence of a military relevance is to be seen in the fencing that bounds the route. The track is set out in a series of dog-legs and, again, unusual for Devon, remains absolutely horizontal for the initial mile.

This plateau-like feature of the landscape is due to the action of an ancient sea-level, many millions of years past, planing off the land surface and providing us today with hilltops that can be categorized according to a specific period in our geological past.

Due to the excellent visibility and lack of tree growth, a monolithic shape soon becomes prominent on the skyline. This is the Brownstone (or Kingswear) daymark and it has graced this spot since 1864. The track will take us to within 100 yards of the structure where a stile and associated pathway across the field have been provided giving access to the daymark to allow closer inspection. The daymark stands 80 feet high and is constructed of local Dartmouth slate. Although built as a utilitarian structure, its artistic lines and octagonal form are in sympathy with the open skyline of land and sea that it surmounts, and it provides a suitable edifice for the river it was built to identify. It was in fact built under the instructions of the newly-formed Dartmouth Harbour Commission, initiated by Charles Seale-Hayne, who was also the landowner of Brownstone. Its construction was only one of the improvements made to facilitate access and navigation into the fast expanding port.

*Brownstone daymark – a nineteenth century signpost to the Dart, visible from all points of the compass.*

Approaching skippers could now look out for the daymark (visible at 20 miles on a good day) and putting that on their starboard bow and the church tower of Stoke Fleming on their port bow the inconspicuous entrance to Dartmouth would open before them.

Leaving the daymark the track now begins its descent towards the cliff-line and the vista of Start Bay opens into a panoramic scene. To our right the occasional gateway breaks the high hedgerow bank and allows us a concentrated view across the river mouth to the coastguard cottages on the Dartmouth side, with Combe Point standing out, together with its accompanying serrated rocks. On a suitable day with a south-westerly breeze blowing, it is a perfect spot to watch the intricate skills required in sailing, as yachts leave the shelter of the land and cant under the power of the gusting wind. It is a reminder of the centuries when sail was the main form of propulsion and how the expertise of a skipper in mastering wind and tide was all-important in making a safe passage.

Above: *The convex open flanks of the eastern shore with Combe Point and the coastguard cottages just visible to the west.*

The track descends to the cliff top at 260 ft (80m) having passed through a kissing gate and joined the South West Coastal Path. Here we find the dispersed buildings of what was once Brownstone Battery, the ultimate destination of that improved track along which we have been walking. The battery was completed in June 1942 and was operated by 556 Coastal Regiment, Royal Artillery. It comprised two 6-inch ex-naval guns with a range of about 25 000 yards (22 750m), and two searchlights. Its main purpose was to deter activity by German E-Boats operating from the Normandy coast. Ironically, considering naval activity in the Channel during the war, its guns were never fired in anger. The only anger incurred seems to have been from the local inhabitants who found their windows shattering every time there was a practice shoot!

Left: *Brownstone Battery with, in the distance, its predecessor, Dartmouth Castle, guarding the narrows.*

On entering the battery area, a level grassy spot, the most conspicuous building, perched right on the edge of the cliff-line, is the Observation Post (OP). A moment to stand (or sit) and stare will confirm for us just why this building was sited here, with 180 degrees of open sea before you and now, in more peaceful times, the steeply dropping, gorse-covered coastline and the Mew Stone standing sentinel to concentrate your gaze. The Mew Stone, one of a number of like-named rocks found around the South West peninsula, which might fancifully be named after the cry of the numerous gulls that are associated with these safe crags, is a perfect habitat and roost for a variety of sea birds. After the gulls, both herring and black-backed, the low-flying, speedy cormorant is a common and recognisable sight here and throughout our journey upriver to Totnes. It is distinguishable from its less common cousin, the shag, by its flash of white breast and the fact that only the cormorant holds out its wings to dry due to having less natural oil in its feathers.

Above: *Searchlight position associated with Brownstone Battery, with the Mew Stone well in range.*

Right: *Inner Froward Point framed by mature Monterey Pines.*

Unlike the steeply dipping, guano-streaked beds of Dartmouth slate of which the Mew Stone is comprised, the headland itself, Inner Froward Point, is constructed of a much harder igneous dolerite rock, better able to withstand the endless battering of those stormy seas. Should time allow it is well worth exploring the area below, accessible along the various paths built at the time of the battery. It is, indeed, a strange phenomena that preservation and conservation of two diametrically opposing facets of life should be brought together here; conservation of a wildlife habitat and preservation of a wartime battery. But that is what we have, and as we make our way between gun emplacements, magazines and searchlight positions, their very presence, immersed in such a variety of natural wildlife, can only help invigorate all the senses in sheer wonderment.

It is an interesting observation that from the inner searchlight position it is possible to see the distant site of Dartmouth Castle, from the last defence to the oldest, a span of 500 years of military evolvement.

Throughout the course of the entire estuary one is constantly reminded of the continuity and timelessness of its being, so much associated through its tidal waters and the life they carry. Today we are excited by the sighting of playful dolphins off the mouth of the river, but even back in 1720 Daniel Defoe 'Had tell of a mighty gathering of dolphins pursuing a great shoal of pilchard up as far as Totnes'. The estuary has much to offer as far as the unexpected is concerned.

From Brownstone Battery, the Coastal Footpath will now provide the line of advance as coastline evolves into river estuary. The path wends its way through and over a variety of topographical settings, from swathes of woodland that clothes the steep shoreline, interspersed with natural balconies providing vistas across the estuary mouth and 'The Range'. The original species of most of the timber in this area, from Inner Froward, round and above Newfoundland Cove, was the salt-resistant Monterey Pine. The gorse-

*Monterey Pines clothe the hillside overlooking Newfoundland Cove.*

covered slopes of the estuary's flanks were planted by Charles Seale-Hayne and like-minded fellow gentry during the latter part of the nineteenth century as part of a move to conserve the area and resist plans for residential development. Today the National Trust have taken on that mantle and the original Montereys, now well thinned by old age and storm, have been supplemented by recent planting of pine and hardwoods.

Having climbed the stile the path once more broadens out to a track-width, carpeted in a soft bed of pine needles, in warm weather the air heavy with the scent of pine. This area was once a rabbit warren during its ownership by such families as the Seale-Haynes and the subsequent 'Warren' names of adjacent properties vouch for this even today. As the track descends a gradual incline, a unique view of the river comes into sight from a very suitable vantage point. This is the point where the waters of the sea converge at the entrance of the river at The Narrows, above which the castles of the Dart were so perfectly sited. Below we see both castles in relationship to each other, Kingswear standing clearly on its bed of blue-grey slate.

*Sunlight glistens on the blue-grey Dartmouth slates, while the twin castles continue to stand sentinel.*

Kingswear Castle was built, slightly later than Dartmouth's second fortification, between 1492 and 1502, but like Dartmouth it was built with gunnery in mind. From our position above it is easy to recognise the effective cross-fire that could be brought to bear on any ship trying to force an entry into the port. However, its south-easterly facing position meant that Kingswear Castle was very much more open to the elements and, especially, breaking seas. The effect of sea spray and salt caused the iron cannon to corrode so rapidly that Sir John Gilbert of Greenway, Governor of the castle, requested bronze replacements in 1578. Cuts in defence spending were just as common as they are today and, with improvements taking place in the

*Proud Kingswear Castle stands erect, seemingly impervious to the constant attack of the sea.*

increasing range of cannon, Kingswear Castle was taken out of commission, with the cannon of Dartmouth able to cover the necessary field of fire. During the Civil War the castle was brought back into use, utilised by both Parliamentarians and Royalist in turn. In later years Charles Seale-Hayne decided to restore the castle as his home, hence also his interest in conserving the surrounding area. One of its last better-known residents of the twentieth century was Sir Fredrick Bennett, MP for Torquay. Today it has been converted into holiday accommodation.

The path is now separated from the estuary by the grounds of Warren Cottage and Warren House until a stepped steep descent of 160 ft (50m) brings us down to very nearly sea level at Mill Bay Cove. As we approach the valley floor castlellated ruins are to be seen perched over the cove adjacent to the entrance to Warren House. It is probable that this was once the site of 'the mill', a building later decorated in gothic style.

The deep, steep-sided valley that the route crosses, is typical of many such valleys, tributaries that feed their individual catchments into the Dart. Having

*A look back at Mill Bay Cove as the route climbs back up to Brownstone.*

crossed the little wooden bridge, with a glimpse of the estuary and passing vessels, it's a steep, zig-zag climb up the north-west valley side to reach the metalled road leading from Kingswear to Home Farm, crossing the entrance drive to Kingswear Castle en-route.

At the top of the climb our route turns right, away from the estuary, to follow the contour of the side valley. A left turn takes the road back into Kingswear village, passing unseen above the site of the Second World War torpedo battery situated below Kingswear Court, and, slightly further upstream, Gommerock, that late medieval fortification that became the anchorage point for the chain on this side of the river. Both sites can only be viewed, either from the Dartmouth shore, near the castle, or, even better, from the river itself.

To complete our circular route the metalled road takes us up as far as Home Farm where the Mill Cove stream is crossed once more and a final ascent of the heights of Brownstone begins. The 400 ft climb is initially a combination of sunken track and dry water-course in summer, but decidedly a running stream in winter. We emerge out on to the hillside adjacent to a brace of Brownstone farmworkers' cottages, now National Trust holiday lets. Having then passed through the neat-and-tidy conglomeration of Brownstone's farm buildings, the open, wind-blown heights and our starting point are once more in sight.

Chapter 3

# *Kingswear Village*

This chapter and walk are dedicated to Kingswear, simply referred to as 'the village' by the locals. Now very much in the shadow of its big sister across the water, Kingswear has played an immensely important part in the development of the port of Dartmouth. In maturity, Kingswear is the elder statesman, as a couplet from a Papal Bull of 1309 states with obvious pride:

*When Kingswear was a market town,*
*Dartmouth was a furzy down.*

*Kingswear.*

Our walk will provide us with the means to identify with much of Kingswear's place in history, now gently lost in the mists of time and changing priorities of life and transport. We start this walk at the heart of 'the village', where the waters of the Dart meet the lower ferry slip – The Square (SX882511). Here much of Kingswear's past life converges in a cacophony of events, some momentous, the vast majority very much more mundane, but interesting still to the vast numbers of visitors who pass this way, including the participants of that stop-go, ant-like procession of the ferry queue, so much part of Kingswear's summer season. We have neither time nor space to here to repeat in detail the rich history of the place, for which any number of dense historical works can be consulted. Instead we just have time to set the scene and drink in the unique atmosphere of this fascinating community.

Above: *Highway over the water, the Lower Ferry, formerly the Horse Ferry.*

Right: *Granite milepost situated on the ferry slip.*

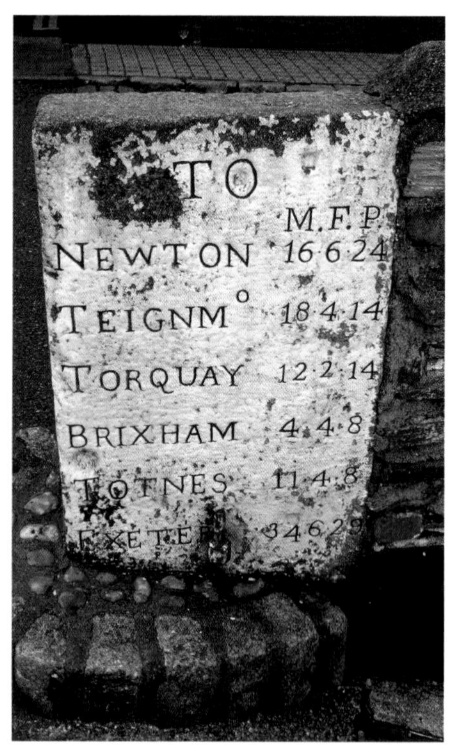


Exploration of the immediate area adjacent to the ferry slip is our first task, and the slip itself holds the initial clue to one of the major reasons for this village coming into being. At the very top of the slip is an ancient granite milepost denoting exact distances in miles, furlongs and poles. Since Norman times, as the port of Dartmouth became a place of real importance, this is where the ancient trackway finished, or began, at the water's edge, having directed the traveller to or from as far as Exeter, or even further afield. A crossing of the 300-yard-wide river here, preceded the port's development by many years. The crossing provides a speedier alternative to the twenty-mile overland route via Totnes, and allowed instant communication between the settlements either side of the river. However it wasn't until 1365 that the Crown acknowledged the importance of this crossing and the provision of a regular ferry service.

The site of the ferry landing at Kingswear was initially slightly further down-river at what is called Collins Quay, a site to which we will return. The landing on the Dartmouth side was at Bearscove, now Bayards Cove. Again, more of this in Chapter 5. The craft used for these early ferries were no more than rowing boats and were for passengers only. Amazingly this simple form of transportation across the river remained until 1840 when the Fownes-Luttrells, owners of the ferry and considerable estates in and around Kingswear, introduced a larger vessel, identified as a 'horse ferry'. Still propelled by 'sweeps' (oars) manned by two men, it could carry one horse-drawn wagon. When observing the tidal currents and power of the river today, we can only marvel at the skill that must have been required to manoeuvre a vessel of this type simply using oars.

During the early 1700s a second 'pulling ferry' was introduced, running from Hoo Down on the northern side of Waterhead Creek across to the 'New Ground' at Dartmouth. The Hoo Down Passage was more accessible for travellers arriving at Kingswear having come on the overland route. An inn, The Passage House, was built for their convenience. The coming of the railway in 1864 saw the demise of the Hoo Down ferry but the introduction of steam power as a revolutionary form of propulsion for the 'horse ferry', came in 1867. Initially owned by the railway company the aptly named *Pioneer* was the forerunner of the lower car ferry today, now owned and run by the Local Authority. The present tugs, by the name of *Hauley*, used to tow the car floats, are descendents of the original *Hauley*, built at Phillips' Yard c.1909.

We'll leave the ferry and railway for our return at the conclusion of this walk and concentrate, once again, on the original reasons for Kingswear's development during earlier centuries. With our backs to the ferry slip, we turn to our right and enter the area known as Kittery. We have a choice of passing immediately under the arch or accessing Priory Street, parallel to the slip. Either will speedily lead us to an abrupt end at a small, peaceful, cobbled slip, adjacent to the Royal Dart Yacht Club, with the gates of Kittery Court immediately ahead of you. We have entered the area of Kingswear that from late Norman times to the seventeenth century, was a centre of trade and commerce, a tightly-knit area of merchants' houses, warehouses and wharves. Kittery Point with its associated Collins Quay (or slip), was the site of many departures from England's shore throughout the centuries. Kingswear ships were licensed in Norman times to transport pilgrims across the Bay of Biscay to La Corunna, en route to the shrine of St James of Compostela, or even further, to

*Collins Quay, Kittery, from where in 1635 Francis Champernowne and Alexander Shapleigh sailed to the New World to set up the first European settlement in Maine, to be named Kittery.*

the Holy Land itself. In addition, with the embarkation of English forces for the 2nd (1147) and 3rd (1190) Crusades taking place from within the sheltered waters of the early port, the movement of pilgrims was considerable and continued well into the fifteenth century. The passage of the *James* of Kingswear, John Heddon, Master, which sailed on 21 January 1434 with forty pilgrims, being one example.

The merchants of Kittery complemented and vied with those of Dartmouth. The port's advantageous geographical position led to a great increase in trade with Bordeaux following the marriage of Henry II to Eleanor of Aquitaine in 1152. During the Hundred Years' War with France, Kingswear provided 13 ships against Dartmouth's 110 for the king's service, in total more than any other port in the country. During the late sixteenth century Richard Kelly, merchant trader of Kingswear is recorded as owning six ships. With the increasing threat from Spain during the reign of Elizabeth I, a survey of qualified mariners available to the country in 1570, found Kingswear able to provide 35 as against 28 from Dartmouth. The community of Kingswear was indeed fulfilling a dynamic part in England's trading and defensive state.

Left and below: *The present-day dwellings and arches of Kittery which have replaced the close-packed buildings of the past.*

Kingswear's influence in England's sixteenth and seventeenth century expansion is just one piece of the Dart estuary's involvement in a jigsaw image that will be further revealed as we proceed upriver. The two important players at this point were the Shapleigh and Champernowne families, related through marriage and trade, and both property owners at Kittery during the early seventeenth century. Between them they financed and initiated the setting up of a new settlement in the Americas, in Maine, at the mouth of the Piscataqua river. In 1635 Francis Champernowne, son of Arthur Champernowne of Dartington, together with Alexander Shapleigh, sailed from Kingswear on the *Benediction* to set up the first European settlement in Maine which they named Kittery!

Other than the little cobbled Collins Slip, complete with its plaque to Kittery, Maine, the Kittery of Kingswear today has little to remind us of those bustling, industrious days set amongst the close-packed buildings and archways. Around 1760, Thomas Fownes, landowner, bought out other property owners of Kittery and set about clearing much of this dockside area, where in its place he built a gentleman's residence, the present Kittery Court. This redevelopment heralded the end of Kingswear as a maritime trading centre and its birth as a residential area for the gentry.

Above and right: *Alma Steps leading up to the Sarah Roope Trust Houses and Room.*

To leave Kittery we find our way to Alma Steps by turning immediately right as we retrace our way along Priory Street. As we climb the steps we are privileged to view the very pleasant gardens of The Priory, a welcome splash of luxuriant green in this still very dense area of dwellings. At the top of the Alma Steps the view is dominated by a striking nineteenth century development constructed of local stone, the Sarah Roope Trust Houses and Room. The Roopes were an influential Kingswear family in Victorian times and later residents of Kittery Court. Sarah Roope, sister of Lieutenant-General Benjamin Roope, endowed the Trust House, providing five dwellings for the needy of the parish, together with a Sunday School Room, now used as a general meeting room for the village.

Kingswear village has developed on a spur of land that protrudes out into the estuary and rises steeply on both sides to 350 ft (115m). To the north the village demarcation consists of Waterhead Creek, with relatively compact development along the valley side. To the south the main stream of the estuary provides the village boundary with rather more grand residences taking advantage of the panoramic setting over the estuary mouth, becoming more dispersed amongst the woodland vegetation that swathes the valley side nearly down to the water's edge. Initially, our route will take us along this southern fringe, so at the top of Alma Steps we turn right along Beacon Road.

For so vertical a landscape this narrow roadway provides a moment of gentle progress as it contours the valley side, enclosed in walls of Dartmouth slate, with residences rising to your left and dipping down to the estuary on your right. The views of the estuary, Warfleet, One Gun Point (better known as the

Gunfield), Gallant's Bower, Dartmouth Castle and St Petrox are accentuated by their appearance, framed between walls and foliage as you proceed. It's worth a mention here of Warfleet, the creek on the opposing bank that divides the castle from the town. Many presume, incorrectly, that the name originated from the Crusader fleets assembling here in the twelfth century. In fact 'fleet' originates from the Saxon word relating to a stream, which in this case flows down the Week valley. Warfleet was an important settlement in its own right during Tudor and Stuart times, with another line of the Roope dynasty very much involved as landowners and merchant adventurers. More recently it had been the site of the successful and popular Dartmouth Potteries, now sadly closed.

*Warfleet, once a independent community lying, with South Town, within the Manor of Stoke Fleming.*

Eventually Beacon Road narrows to a pathway as another panoramic view-point of the estuary mouth emerges. Below, on the foreshore can be seen the successor of the1864 lighthouse, constructed to replace St Petrox light and to improve the night-time approach to the port. Just a few yards past the light can be seen a recently-built residence on the site of an old boathouse, its construction controversial in the extreme, considering its position. The effects of the local mild and humid climate are very apparent in this small recess of

the river estuary, plant life displaying semi-tropical characteristics, evident even during the winter months. Situated between Beacon Road and Beacon Lane, again well camouflaged behind drapes of foliage, is the grand residence of The Beacon. This house was built in 1845 for Governor Arthur Howe Holdsworth, one of the most influential men of Victorian Dartmouth and Kingswear, and last Governor of Dartmouth Castle. For eighteen years he was MP for Dartmouth, twice being its Mayor. He was responsible for the creation of the River Dart Steam Navigation Company, providing the first steamboat service between Dartmouth and Totnes in 1837 and, just before his death, he became a major shareholder in the Dartmouth & Torbay Railway Company.

A few more steps up the rise brings us to the junction of Beacon Road with Castle Road which we will follow for approximately 300 yards when we arrive at the rear of Brookhill. This beautiful house with its associated grounds spreading down to the water's edge, is best viewed from the estuary, or from the Dartmouth side, close by Dartmouth Castle. Rebuilt in its present position in 1825 it was the Holdsworth residence prior to the building of The Beacon. Before being converted into flats in the late twentieth century it had provided accommodation for a number of illustrious persons, among them Napoleon III and, during the Second World War, the future President Mitterand of France, who was billeted here as a member of the Free French Naval Squadron operating Motor Torpedo Boats out of the port.

Above: *The Beacon, built for Governor Arthur Howe Holdsworth in 1845. Below the successor to the 1864 navigation light, constructed to ease night entry into the port.*

Right: *Brookhill, Governor Holdsworth's earlier residence and home to Free French Naval personnel during the Second World War.*

This area of Kingswear is often referred to as Fountain Violet, after the farm situated at the head of the combe above Brookhill. For our exploration of Kingswear we will now briefly retrace our steps for one hundred yards along the Castle Road before turning up a right-of-way to our right, through a pair of well-weathered, but once elegant gateposts. First impressions would suppose this to be a private driveway but a half-hidden finger post will confirm our right to climb the hill towards Fountain Violet Farm. Passing an attractive but isolated cottage on our right, we immediately follow the route left through a gate and on to the farm's main drive and on up to the top of the Kingwear ridge and the junction with the Mount Ridley Road, 350 ft above sea level. As we climb so fine views of the estuary will present themselves, an obvious incentive for a previous generation who sited the delicate, now ruinous, ivy-clad, wooden and brick chalet, close by Fountain Violet Farm.

Turn left down Mount Ridley Road which follows the spine of the ridge. To our left, now a well-obscured residential development, once stood the Redoubt, constructed during the Civil War to protect the Kingswear approaches to the port and complementing its Dartmouth twin at Gallant's Bower. Its dominating position will soon become apparent as we begin our descent of Redoubt Hill. Have a thought for Sir Henry Carey of Cockington and his men when surrender of this position to Fairfax was finally agreed during the winter of 1646.

Our descent winds down the steep ridge providing one of the best views of the main anchorage (the 'Pool' as it is sometimes known) of the port where fleets have anchored since the days of the Crusades, to the great assembly for the D-Day landings of June 1944. Today the fleet is very much more peaceful in intent, comprising sailing and other leisure craft of all sizes and states of sophistication. From here the estuary can be seen wending its way inland and in the far distance, on a clear day, the hills of Dartmoor, from whence the Dart is born.

From Ridley Hill, we turn once more to make the final steep descent down Church Hill to its junction with Beacon Road and there, on the opposite side of the road, stands the Church of St Thomas of Canterbury, its clean, grey stone structure solidly cut into the hillside, a lasting symbol of the continuity of life here for the past thousand years. The squat church tower, medieval in origin, is the oldest part of the building, the remainder having been reconstructed during the 1840s. Beside the church, on Higher Street (previously known as

*The Pool, where for centuries fleets have gathered, from the Crusades of the twelfth century to the embarkation for D-Day in 1944. Today the fleet is of a more peaceful character with leisure and recreation its intent.*

*The Church of St Thomas of Canterbury, long-standing symbol of the village of Kingswear.*

The Plains) stands the Ship Inn, partially enclosed by a cluster of terraced cottages, all providing the nucleus of the original village, safely set 50 feet up above the river. Walk on up Higher Street to join Fore Street at what is called the Banjo, the most recent addition to the village's road infrastructure to improve the flow of traffic. From here there is a grandstand view of the harbour once more, and immediately below the line of Waterhead Creek, the railway terminus and Dartside Marina. It is on the banks of the creek that the wooden hulls of Kingswear ships were once built, ships such as the 14-ton sloop *Good Intent* in 1784, the 30-ton sloop *Start* in the 1840s, and the 154-ton *Mizpah* in the 1850s.

The building slips disappeared under the new railway sidings with the arrival of the Dartmouth & Torbay Railway in 1864. We will mention more of the coming of the railway and its influence on Kingswear and the port in Chapter 6. At this juncture, looking down on this thriving private railway, how lucky for the community and tourism, that with the demise of the main-line link to London with Beeching's axe, the Dart Valley Railway Company took control of the line from Paignton to Kingswear on 1 January 1973. Having initially run the line under the aegis of the Torbay Steam Railway, it is now the Paignton & Dartmouth Steam Railway.

Now walking down Fore Street, in front of the station building, we arrive back at our starting point at the Square and Lower Ferry slip. The dominant building here, between slip and station, is the Royal Dart Hotel. This hotel was built under the direction of Charles Seale-Hayne with the arrival of the railway. Its purpose was to provide accommodation for railway passengers awaiting the arrival of their ship for onward journeys across the Atlantic, or to any one of the four corners of the British Empire. One of the major purposes for building the railway was to stimulate the development of Dartmouth as a major transatlantic sea port, and many of the local gentry such as Seale-Hayne, were prepared to invest in this vision. A rather touching symbol of that era, and later, is the elegant Italianate clock tower complete with the nostalgic lettering – GWR.

During the Second World War the Royal Dart Hotel was to have other duties to perform when its upper storeys were taken over by the Royal Navy and it became HMS *Cicala*, an operational command centre for up to seven flotillas of Motor Torpedo Boats (MTBs), Motor Gun Boats (MGBs), and Motor Launches (MLs) working out of the estuary. Amongst their number was a Free

*Kingswear: the railway terminus and the Royal Dart Hotel. Both railway and hotel epitomize the energy, determination and confidence that characterised Victorian society.*

French flotilla, hence the use of Brookhill as crew quarters. The diverse objectives of the flotillas included convoy duties in the Channel and hit-and-run raids off the French coast. The 15th Motor Gunboat Flotilla was involved in very much more clandestine operations such as ferrying agents to and from the Brittany coast, liaising with Resistance fighters and picking up escaped Allied airmen. The bravery and skill required by these crews in carrying out their tasks off an enemy coast cannot be over-emphasised. It is then particularly harrowing that the last casualty of the flotilla should occur literally as the war was coming to an end, and not off France but the Norwegian coast. MGB 502 was lost on 12 May 1945 with only two survivors picked up. The 15th Flotilla is commemorated on a plaque to be seen on the ferry slip, together with an inscription in the Church of St Thomas of Canterbury which also holds in remembrance the White Ensign last flown by MGB 502.

From Kingswear we will now make our way across the estuary to follow in the footsteps of the dignitaries and merchants of Dartmouth.

Chapter 4

# *Clifton – Dartmouth – Hardness*

Dartmouth's hereditary title, still used at times of elections, gives emphasis to its pedigree and the fact that it is a 'coming together' of diverse settlements. The very name - Dartmouth - with which we identify the town today informs us as to where it has come from, the mouth, the very waters of the Dart itself. Rising sea levels following the end of the last Ice Age deprived the early inhabitants of this area of any flat land adjacent to the river. The hills dipped down steeply into tidal waters, with the main river channel indented with three steep-sided creeks whose present-day names are Warfleet, Old Mill, and, the site of where Dartmouth town lies today. One thousand years ago, nearly every yard of flat, low-lying land that makes up the town of Dartmouth today would have been underwater at high tide. The town has grown out of the river itself.

The gradual development and historical importance of Dartmouth from its initial natural state provides us with any number of historic and visual jewels. We are fortunate that a number of these lie in close proximity to one another owing to Dartmouth's very compactness. For this chapter you will simply amble amongst the buildings and streets, allowing yourself freedom to dip into the fascinations of old Dartmouth. To give some cohesiveness to your exploration, a chronological guide will suffice to set out the story of Dartmouth's development, looking at specific areas and buildings relevant to each period of history.

The seed of Dartmouth was sown by the Saxons with their creation of a farming settlement high up above the river and creek at Townstal (Tunstal). Here they were nearer to more manageable land and a safe distance from the river below from where possible Viking attacks could ensue. Your walk associated with Chapter 7 will pass through this area of original Dartmouth providing an opportunity to identify aspects of its individuality and setting.

The attraction of the river estuary as a natural harbour was immediately recognised by the Normans. Embarkation for the two crusades of 1147 and 1190 took advantage of boarding facilities along the water's edge. The increased trade between England and Bordeaux, brought about by the marriage of Henry II and Eleanor of Aquitaine, added to the success of the port. Quays and the provision of a whole host of artisan skills required in a maritime world began to develop along the foreshore – shipwrights, sailmakers, rope-makers, coopers, blacksmiths, prevalent amongst them. Housing for these craftsmen and their families also needed to be close at hand and so we begin to see the development of two settlements, either side of the main creek. To the north of the creek a ridge of land descends from Townstal to the water's edge, in those days protruding out into the main stream. This nose (or ness) of land became the site for both housing and workshops, and became known as Hardness. To the south of the main creek a separate settlement developed under the steep hillside (or cliff). This became known as Clifton. Even centuries later the limpet-like characteristics of Clifton's dwellings were a point of interest to travellers, as the Reverend John Swete observed in 1792.

*I was highly delighted with the appearance of the town*
*which seemed to rise out of the river, and wanting space to expatiate on,*
*had occupied the steep side of the hill behind – fixing its houses on ledges*
*of rock and hanging apparently pensile from it.*

Initially Clifton and Hardness were separated by the creek and to communicate with each other, other than by boat, a walk was required around the head of the creek, crossing the valley at the fording place. The importance of the ford and the tracks joining Clifton and Hardness to it, are evidenced in the fact that associated place and road names still remain today. The positioning of ford and the topography of the land make it relatively easy to identify the site the original creek, with North and South Ford Roads running down either side of the flat, reclaimed creek.

By 1243 a physical means of bridging the creek had been constructed, but initially this was in order to provide a site for two tidal water mills. This was the building of a dam, or Foss, and today it provides us with the line of Foss Street. The creek became an immense mill pool, stretching from the ford down

Above: *Ford, where once the stream at the head of the creek was crossed.*

Left: *Clifton, fronted by Bayards Cove, originally Bear's Cove.*

to the Foss. With technological improvements over the centuries, these mills continued in use until the early nineteenth century with the Foss itself providing a thoroughfare, bringing the inhabitants of Clifton and Hardness together as the town of Dartmouth. On the river side of the Foss quays and warehouses developed, fronting immediately on to the river.

With England's developing trade with the Biscay ports, Dartmouth was well positioned to take full advantage of the situation, both in peace and war. Wine became the most important import, conveyed in well adapted, rather rotund looking craft, named 'cogs'. Their propulsion was a single square sail with simple superstructures both fore and aft, particularly useful in warfare and aptly named 'castles' – hence the later terminology forecastle or fo'c'sle. The importance of these vessels became so important to Dartmouth that they became the centrepiece in the town's Coat of Arms. In return, Dartmouth and its hinterland had much to export to the European mainland. Dartmoor tin was highly sought-after and the river made a most suitable export highway from Totnes. Woollen cloth and fish were two other major commodities that would add to the prosperity of Dartmouth as a sea port.

*Foss Street, marking the line of the ancient dam (foss) that once joined Hardness and Clifton into one town.*

By 1327 Dartmouth's importance was without question, so when presented with both town and waters of the port by a grateful subject, Nicholas of Tewskesbury, Edward III provided the town with the status of Royal Borough. Eleven years later he in turn presented the Waters of the Dart (and much more) to his son, the Black Prince, The Duke of Cornwall. From that day to this the Dart estuary had remained Duchy property.

The Dartmouth family that best reflect this period of Dartmouth's history, are the Hawleys. Originating from the Tuckenhay area, John Hawley had constructed for himself both warehouse and quay on the Foss by 1344. Having brought the family to Dartmouth it was his son and grandson, John II and III who would be identified with the period as leading merchants, landowners and privateers of medieval Dartmouth.

At one period, John Hawley II possessed a dozen ships, being just one of 25 shipowners in the town. Their ability to create wealth for the town brought them close to the wind in their relationship with the king, often crossing the fine line drawn between privateering (legal piracy) and blatant piracy!

Having probably been instrumental in the Breton aggravation in the first place, it was John Hawley II who oversaw the building of the fortalice and the positioning of a chain at the mouth of the river to defend the town.

John II was mayor of Dartmouth nine times and both father and son were Members of Parliament in their respective periods. Their impressive timber-framed residence, befitting their status, lay between Higher and Lower Streets, in Clifton, a type of house now best represented by the fourteenth-century Merchant's House in Higher Street, now the Cherub Inn. It is interesting that the influential period of the Hawleys coincides with the Hundred Years' War (1338–1453) during which the port of Dartmouth provided more ships to the service of the king than any other in the country. Dartmouth's robust sea-faring reputation seems to have been well known at this time as it is thought that Geoffrey Chaucer's 'schipman of Dert-e-mouthe' drew on an amalgam of characteristics associated with certain ships' masters of Dartmouth.

John Hawley II was laid to rest in the, then, recently constructed Church of St Saviour's in 1408. Buried in the chancel, a magnificent brass, showing him in knight's armour, accompanied by his two wives, is a fitting memorial to the man who led the town in its aggressive drive to commercial success. He was

Far left: *The fourteenth-fifteenth century Church of St Saviour. The spiritual and cultural core of Dartmouth's community over the centuries.*

Left: *The fourteenth century Merchant's House in Higher Street, now The Cherub Inn.*

also much involved in providing funds for the building of the town's new church. Much patience and perseverance had been required from the time of its conception in 1286 when Edward I, on a visit to the town, was petitioned to permit a new chapel to be built to serve the new town at the bottom of the hill, thus saving the parishioners the long walk up to Townstal and the Church of St Clements. In 1372, nearly ninety years later, the chapel of Holy Trinity was dedicated, being licensed in 1400 in the name of St Mary, finally taking the name of St Saviour's by 1416. As with so many Devon towns and villages, its sturdy grey-blue slate structure stands as a symbol of the town's spiritual and commercial life and continuity, visible from most quarters of its tightly-packed community.

Initially the water's edge at Clifton lay along the line of the Quay (in front of the Royal Castle Hotel), Fairfax Place and Lower Street. By Tudor times, a curving line of just a few additional yards of reclamation from the Quay to Bayards Cove was in place, this providing land for warehouses and wharves abutting immediately on to the river frontage. The quay at Bayards Cove is

first mentioned in the sixteenth century. In those days its name was Bears Cove, possibly a reference to the fact that bear baiting was held there. The circular battery at the end of the quay was built around 1539, during the reign of Henry VIII, as a second line of defence, should enemy ships have broken through the defensive chain at the mouth of the river. It was not until the nineteenth century that battery and quay were linked together. Today Bayards Cove provides the only example of a quayside with characteristics relating back to those earlier days. However, its pristine appearance today belies the cacophony of sounds, the variety of aromas, and the hectic activity that must have accompanied the bustle of a busy port.

Above: *The old quay of Bayards Cove, once Bears Cove, with its eighteenth century Customs House centrepiece.*

Right: *On the southern extremity of Bayards Cove, sits its defensive bulwark, built during the reign of Henry VIII.*

It is on the quay at Bayards Cove that the memorial plaque to the Pilgrim Fathers is situated. It was in August 1620 that the *Mayflower* and *Speedwell* came into Dartmouth in order that the *Speedwell* could be repaired before continuing their journey to the New World. In fact the ships had once more to make port in England due to further leaks in the *Speedwell*. Returning to Plymouth, the decision was made to leave the *Speedwell* behind and proceed in the *Mayflower* alone. It is thought that sabotage by members of the crew was the cause the leaks in her sister ship. It is an interesting conjecture that if

*The New World awaits! The stone commemorating the sailing of the* Mayflower *(and* Speedwell*) in August 1620, situated at Bayards Cove.*

Dartmouth had been the last port of call of the Pilgrim Fathers then Dartmouth, New England would have been the site of the founding American settlement, not Plymouth.

One of the buildings situated on Bayards Cove is the site of the old Customs House. The present building was converted from four small cottages in 1737 to provide accommodation for this important service to the Crown. It highlights the strategic position that Dartmouth gained in the registration and collection of customs dues on goods entering and leaving, not only the port of Dartmouth, but Totnes and all the harbours from Torbay down to the mouth of the Yealm, near Plymouth.

Tudor and Stuart times for Dartmouth would see the importance of the Newfoundland cod trade dominate all others. The building which exemplifies this period more than any other is The Butterwalk, in Duke Street. Although cod was being caught off Newfoundland early on in the sixteenth century, it was the taking of the island in the name of Queen Elizabeth I by Sir Humphrey Gilbert in 1583 that provided the catalyst for a trade that was important to Dartmouth for the next 200 years. Each March, a migration of many hundreds

*The Butterwalk. Symbol of the successful Newfoundland cod fishery of Tudor and Stuart times.*

of seamen from the towns and villages of South Devon sailed from Dartmouth and other ports, three thousand miles across the Atlantic to Newfoundland. Here they set up homes in roughly constructed dwellings of stone and timber. During the day some then fished for the abundant cod from small dories using long-lines. Each catch was then prepared by workers on shore; gutting, cleaning and racking the filleted fish to dry. When ready the dried fish was salted down in barrels. In addition the highly valuable cod liver oil, known as 'train oil' was collected. At the end of the season the fully laden ships returned to Europe, often to the Catholic ports of Spain or Portugal, where a better price could be obtained for the dried cod. Other sought-after produce, such as spices, dried fruits, wine or Spanish iron, was purchased for the English market and from the proceeds of their sale the merchants of Dartmouth prospered and built themselves refined town houses such as are seen in the Butterwalk. To the rear were their warehouses and quays with the waters of the Dart lapping up to the line of the Foss. This annual migration provided ready employment for thousands of Westcountry folk, but at a cost when considering those ships that were lost at sea. As the years progressed, a proportion of families decided to set up home on Newfoundland and so began the original twinning of such town names as Dartmouth and Torbay.

Although no longer residences of the merchant classes, we are fortunate in having access to view the internal architecture and décor of the Stuart Period through the businesses and services that now make up the Butterwalk. Especially worth a visit are Dartmouth Museum and the aptly named 'Sloping Deck Restaurant'. It was within a panelled room of the present museum that Charles II was welcomed by the Mayor of Dartmouth on 23 July 1671. It was this year also that work was proceeding on the next stage of reclaiming more of the river – what was to be called the 'New Ground'. Identified today by the garden area containing the bandstand, it was originally a manmade island contained by a stone wall, useful as an additional area of quayside and joined to Duke Street by a bridge.

*The town's bandstand is situated on the 'New Ground', land reclaimed in the seventeenth century.*

It is extraordinary to realize that one of Dartmouth's most famous sons, Thomas Newcomen, was born in the same century as that of the building of the Butterwalk. A practical ironmonger by trade he became an inventor and creator of the first atmospheric steam engine. A preliminary scale model was successfully constructed in his workshop in Dartmouth by 1710, the first full-scale working engine being built within the South Staffordshire coalfield, near Dudley Castle in 1712, its job to pump water out of the mine. The descendant of Newcomen's steam engine was to return to the port of Dartmouth in the nineteenth century to play a vital role, both on land and sea, in revitalising trade and providing employment. Sadly Newcomen's house in Lower Street was demolished in 1864 to make way for an improved roadway to South Town, rightly named Newcomen Road. In 1963 a surviving Newcomen steam engine was brought back to the town and it can be seen in a purpose-built building attached to the Tourist Information Centre in Mayor's Avenue.

By the early nineteenth century much of the town had deteriorated due to recession and the unsightly state of the mill pool, now largely silted up, was a decided health risk, especially during the summer months. To the rescue came Arthur Howe Holdsworth, MP for the town, benefactor and landed gentry. He was responsible for obtaining an Improvement Act in 1815 which saw the final demise of the tidal mill and the filling in of the mill pool. On its site, adjacent to Foss Street, the Pannier Market was built in 1828–29. For overland transportation of goods the steep hillsides to and from Dartmouth had once only allowed horse transport, with pannier baskets attached. With the Improvement Act also came the laying out and building of a 'New' road, later named Victoria Road, leading up to Townstal, and with a gradient accessible to horse-drawn carriages and carts.

*The picturesque Pannier Market, constructed 1828–29 and still providing a regular focal point for the surrounding rural community.*

To the north of Foss Street lies the old shoreline etched out by Broadstone and Undercliff. The sweep of Mayor's Avenue mirrors this line and between the two lay the major boat-building slips of Hardness. Now partially overlaid by Plymco Supermarket, this is the area where ships had been built from the twelfth to the nineteenth century, from small trading vessels to men-of-war associated with the Napoleonic Wars.

This stage of our exploration of Dartmouth is completed by returning to what is referred to today as the Boat Float, an area of enclosed water, now only accessible to small boats (more of this in Chapter 6). In Tudor times a 'New Quay' was constructed here to provide for the increasing Newfoundland cod trade. Two prominent merchants' houses were built on the quay, known today as the Royal Castle Hotel. By the end of the eighteenth century the merchants' houses had become the Castle Inn, complete with brewhouse and stables. Over the years it has provided refreshment and a bed for gentlemen of literary and artistic excellence such as Daniel Defoe in 1720, The Reverend John Swete during the 1790s, and William Turner in 1811 and again in 1814. Its regal guests in the name of the Prince of Wales (Edward VII) and his sons, provided the legitimacy of a Royal prefix by 1902, to be followed by later Royal Princes.

*The Royal Castle Hotel proudly overlooks the Boat Float, an open quayside until the building of the South Embankment in 1885.*

Chapter 5

# *Waterfronts and Ferries*

As we have already observed, the port of Dartmouth comprises an area of water bounded on two sides by the town of Dartmouth and the village of Kingswear. A commendable way to view the harbour area and bring the history of this delightful area up to date is to circumnavigate the whole, taking in both waterfronts and two more ferry crossings.

Your walk will start outside Dartmouth's Tourist Information Centre (SX878515), adjacent to the main town car park, off Mayor's Avenue. This is a very appropriate place to begin as it continues the story of Dartmouth's development from the previous chapter. Prior to 1883 you would have been submerged by the high tide at this spot, or up to your waist in river mud at low tide. This area was also referred to as the Pool, and would have seen ships either manoeuvring for the various wharves abutting New Ground, New Quay and The Foss, or perhaps utilising the shipyards close at hand. By 1883 the Pool area had deteriorated so much it was decided to fill it in and finally bring to an end centuries of river access and boat-building to this central area of Dartmouth. Mayor's Avenue was built on this newly reclaimed land, all of this work being the initial stages of development associated with the Dartmouth Harbour Improvement Bill of 1881.

Mayor's Avenue leads you round and on to the Embankment, later referred to as the South Embankment. There is no doubt that the Victorians were the great constructors and innovators of the age, and Dartmouth's imaginative development mirrored what was happening throughout the country and Empire. Its 600-yard length ran from the Lower Ferry slip to just north of its junction with Mayor's Avenue, where the town's Victorian gasworks were situated at the foot of Hardness. Its brainchild and architect was Samuel Lake,

*The Port of Dartmouth, a seemingly land-locked stretch of water – the perfect natural harbour.*

a highly respected engineer and designer of ships and ports. Its construction, completed in 1885, saw the irregular medieval and Tudor waterfront, finally erased forever, replaced by the clean lines of its much more accessible successor. Not that its arrival came unopposed! When walking or driving along the Embankment today one is oblivious to the bad feeling and bitterness that arose during this major restructuring of Dartmouth's waterfront. The objectors to the scheme were led by Francis Simpson, Rear Commodore of the newly-formed Royal Dart Yacht Club, but also a boatyard owner who was about to see his yard cut off from the river. It is ironic that Simpson should have taken this attitude in some ways as he was to play no small part in driving through change affecting his new yard across the river at Noss (more of which in Chapter 7). The working classes of the town were encouraged to join the objectors with the threat that the Embankment would cause a substantial increase in the price of coal. There is no doubt that this *cause célebre* threw up some interesting bedfellows! The only sign left of that previous era of Dartmouth's maritime past is what is referred to as the Boat Float, a quayside now cut off from the river, except for very small boats. The quay immediately in front of the Royal Castle Hotel originated as the 'New Quay' and the northern arm as a constituent part of the seventeenth-century 'New Ground'.

*The original Embankment now extended and heightened during the 1980s to prevent flooding.*

*New Ground, now a social gathering place for locals and visitors alike, overlooking the Boat Float.*

Our route is now a brief walk north to the Higher Car Ferry. Once again though, within a very few yards, the influence of the landscape over the town's development becomes apparent. The South Embankment merges into the North Embankment under that nose of land, Hardness, but yet the North Embankment was not completed until 1937. As you approach the Higher Ferry slip notice how a flat, semi-circular area of land opens up to your left, with College Way striking away up the hill towards Townstal, at right angles to the river. Once again you have an area of reclaimed land, once named Coombe Mud and infilled behind the North Embankment in 1937. In its tidal past it possessed shipyards on its southern flank, under Hardness, whilst later the area was often chosen as a ship's graveyard and amongst the remains, now buried under what is today Coronation Park, lies the carcass of a British submarine. Coombe Road flanks the northern rim of Coronation Park as it once flanked Coombe Mud. Still standing is Coombe Terrace, built in 1870 by Samuel Lake, of South Embankment fame, unique in that they are the first preformed concrete houses built in the United Kingdom. Taken from the river, Coronation Park today provides a vital area of flat open space for the town.

*Coombe Terrace, built in 1870. The first preformed concrete houses built in the United Kingdom.*

The northernmost point of Coombe Mud, where the ferry slip is today, began the area known as Sandquay. Following a considerable argument on rights of ownership, much repeated over the years between landowner, Corporation and Duchy, John Seale completed the building of a major shipbuilding area by the late 1700s, an industry that would continue for the next 200 years. During the Napoleonic Wars sixteen ships were built here for the Royal Navy, including a frigate named after the town itself. In 1858 a relative newcomer to Dartmouth from Scotland, George Philip, took over the Sandquay Yards and so began a long association of the Philip name related to boat-building and repairs. In 1896 the first all-steel boat to be built on the river took to the water from Sandquay. She was the *Totnes Castle*, one of the fleet of paddle steamers that plied the river between Totnes and Dartmouth. In 1965 Philip & Son sold their Dart yards to Reeves, timber merchants based at Totnes. They then closed down the Sandquay yard, utilising the area as a small marina and converting the office block into the Dart Marina Hotel.

*Sandquay, once the site of considerable shipbuilding, including Philip & Son's Yard, now the location of the Dart Marina Hotel with its adjacent marina.*

As influential owner of Sandquay it was John Henry Seale who initiated the creation of the Higher Ferry in 1831. Providing easier overland access to Dartmouth had been sought for some years and with the development of the turnpikes the river was a barrier the authorities wished to overcome. Initially a suspension bridge was proposed across the river at the Dittisham Narrows, but due to determined opposition by James Marwood Elton, owner of the Greenway Estate and ferry, this initiative was shelved. The influence of Greenway owners over the years, relating to river crossings, has had an immense influence on the development of the lower Dart valley and the surrounding area of the South Hams.

Seale now proceeded with his initiative and, following an Act of Parliament, a floating bridge was positioned joining Sandquay to the new road leading to and from Hillhead and hence to Newton Abbot and Exeter. The term 'floating bridge' relates to the fact that the ferry was attached to the shore by chains which guided the vessel on its crossing. Later models would see a single chain replaced by two wire hawsers. When first installed in 1831 the 'floating bridge' was powered by a steam engine but due to this being too costly to run, it was replaced by two horses who worked a treadmill to power the ferry – literally, two horsepower! This very basic form of propulsion continued until 1867 when the new owners of the ferry, Philip & Son, built a new steam-powered ferry. The first ferry carried four carriages as a full load, or a flock of sheep, or herd of cattle – presumably not together! One of the first, and relatively few Royal users of the ferry was Princess Victoria, who at the age of 14 passed this way en-route from Plymouth to Torquay in order to avoid the seasickness associated with a sea voyage.

*The Higher Car Ferry, which began operations in 1831. Due to its contact with the land in the form of guiding cables it is officially registered as a floating bridge.*

The present Higher Ferry came into service in 1960 bringing with it the demise of hissing steam power and throbbing pistons and the introduction of the far less attractive diesel engines, which continue to power both locals and holidaymakers across the river.

Whilst crossing on the Higher Ferry, especially as a foot passenger, it is the ideal moment to introduce the arrival of Britannia and the commencement of Dartmouth as the home of Officer-Cadet training for the Royal Navy. Looking immediately upriver from the ferry, this area of water was the site of permanent anchorage for HMS *Britannia*, arriving September 1863, to be joined in 1864 by HMS *Hindustan*. *Britannia*'s arrival was greeted by cheering crowds and the ringing of church bells. These two wooden-walled ships, relics of the days of naval power in the days of Nelson, were to be rugged home and school to in excess of 200 officer-cadets between the ages of 12 and 16. The vessels remained on station for 53 years. In January 1877 The Prince of Wales (to become King Edward VII) brought his two sons, George and Edward, down by train to join Britannia, thus starting a tradition of Royal association with the Royal Navy and Dartmouth. It seems that Royal status was no guarantee of respect for the young boys who would have to put up with the miseries inflicted by bullying. For the Princes' arrival in 1877 a temporary miniature station was built immediately adjacent to the railway level-crossing at the ferry landing slip. In fact this 'temporary' structure continued in use for many years, specifically for use by officer-cadets. It became known as Britannia Halt, but sadly no longer exists. It was situated immediately opposite the little signal box by the crossing.

By the end of the nineteenth century, pressures brought about by the needs of a radically changing navy and deteriorating health problems within the cramped conditions on board the hulks, saw plans drawn up and funds allocated for the building of a shore establishment. The first building to be completed was the hospital for the ever- increasing needs of sick cadets. Then on 7 March 1902 King Edward VII laid the foundation stone of the main block of what was to become Britannia Royal Naval College. Designed by Aston Webb, the initial building was ready for use in September 1905 but it was not until 1918 that all the building requirements were completed to cope with the 400 cadets making up the full complement. In those early years of the new century BRNC was to be the second stage in an Officer-Cadet's training. Following two years at Osborne House, on the Isle of Wight, they would then come on to Dartmouth to complete their land education before joining their ships as midshipmen at the age of 16. It is a sobering thought that with the

*Britannia Royal Naval College, opened September 1905.*

outbreak of the First World War the entire intake from Dartmouth was allocated posts on His Majesties Ships and within 12 months many had already perished due to U-Boat activity in the North Sea.

In its early years Webb's design, in its raw state, was not always admired as much as it is now. There were those who likened it to an asylum or work-house! Time and maturing grounds have mellowed its appearance on the hillside above the river. Being a Naval Establishment the traditions of the Royal Navy and shipboard life play their part in the character of the college. The thread that ties the main building together is a magnificent barrelled ceiling corridor terminating in the Chapel at one end and the Senior Gunroom at the other. Centre stage is the Quarterdeck with its surrounding Poop Deck. The Quarterdeck is directly accessible from the Parade Ground through the main doors of the College. On the Parade Ground stands a reconstructed ship's figurehead of Britannia, a link with the college's origins down on the river. BRNC is a fascinating mix today of the great traditions of the Senior Service, still overlooked and inspired by 'the Nelson touch', and the awesome technology and power of a modern, if decidedly smaller Navy.

*The reconstructed ship's figurehead of Britannia which once graced the bow of His Britannic Majesty's man-of-war.*

However, the number of officer-cadets remains constant, although now recruited at a considerably higher age and from a variety of countries. For Dartmouth it provides an continuing prestigious identity and a source of substantial employment and income for the town.

Tours of the Royal Naval College can be arranged through Dartmouth Tourist Information Centre.

Down on the water, launches, sailing dinghies and yachts provide the appropriate experiences for officer cadets. These are based and serviced from the northern end of Sandquay, where occasionally larger naval craft might be seen on a visit to the port.

Having landed from the Higher Ferry on the Kingswear side, take the footpath situated between the railway line and the river. We are now going to follow the railway line on the final stage of its journey that once originated for many at Paddington in London. The Dartmouth & Torbay Railway Company were the builders of this line. The 14 March 1861 saw the line opened as far as

*The original Dartmouth & Torbay Railway passes by Sir Henry Seale's higher ferry slip.*

Churston Station (known as Brixham Road in those days) but finances were rapidly running out. The original estimate for the work from Torquay to Dartmouth was £90 000, the final costs totalling over £260 000. Churston to Kingswear was the last section to be completed and would take another three years. The financial saviour of this last stretch of line was the setting up of the Dart Harbour Commission between 1861 and 1863. In response to positive enquiries from two shipping lines to use port facilities, the new Commission allowed additional funds to be raised to complete the railway and improve harbour facilities. Charles Seale-Hayne, a railway director, was the prime mover in this cause with his uncle, Sir Henry Seale, being the owner of the Higher Ferry. At one stage he was very keen to see the railway terminate at the Higher Ferry slip so that his ferry and pocket would be the beneficiaries.

The construction of the line initially, but briefly, halted at Hoodown, on the northern side of Waterhead Creek. Today, this spot is marked by the gated crossing traversing the line. The slip within close proximity marks the end of the road from where the early eighteenth century Hoodown 'pulling' ferry left the Kingwear shore for the New Ground of Dartmouth. An inn was situated here for travellers, at one time known as The Passage House. With the arrival of the railway, Fownes-Luttrell, owner of both Kingswear ferries and also a director of the railway company, sold the ferry rights to the railway together with the appropriate land necessary to extend the line across the creek and up to the village of Kingswear. During the Second World War a torpedo store was sited here to provide munitions for the MTB flotillas working out of the river.

On 10 August 1864 the first passenger train arrived at a very basic Kingswear Station, 6½ years after the first sod was cut at Torre Station, Torquay. Funds and

*Footpath and railway hug the river bank providing a superb view of estuarine life and activity for walker and passenger alike.*

grants raised through the newly floated Dart Harbour Commission saw the completion of the station and associated buildings, a new deepwater quay provided, and additional navigational aids positioned. With Seale-Hayne's new Royal Dart Hotel constructed, the infrastructure was in place to launch Dartmouth harbour as a transatlantic, even world-wide port, one of the major objectives for the building of the railway line in the first place.

Other than the fact that the harbour was a safe, deepwater anchorage, two further amenities were now sought: Dartmouth as a mailing station and Dartmouth as a coaling port, one often attracting the other. Steamships required large quantities of coal with which to top up their bunkers before leaving the British Isles for the four corners of the Empire. With coal being brought round by ship from the South Wales coalfields and stored in coal hulks, this trade began to flourish. 1890 was the peak year with 747 ships calling in to coal. Gangs of men, identified as 'lumpers' had the job of loading the coal, a dirty and back-breaking job, often using shovel, basket and barrow. Work was highly competitive with representatives of each gang racing each other to the quayside from various vantage points such as Gallant's Bower to win the right to load a ship. The rate of pay for many years around the turn of the nineteenth and twentieth centuries was 2d a ton. No work – no pay! Many lived in tenements along the Dartmouth waterfront area, often 15 families in one house, the Victorian slums of Dartmouth. Finally the appalling state of these homes between the two World Wars saw the first stages of new Council housing at Townstal – Dartmouth's development had gone full-circle.

*The Italianate tower of Charles Seale-Hayne's Royal Dart Hotel, with its now incomplete memorial to the time-keeping qualities of God's Wonderful Railway!*

The competition for winning mailing contracts was a great deal harder to come by. It wasn't until 1871 that Dartmouth won a contract with the Cape & Natal Steam Navigation Company for their ships to call on a monthly basis to pick up, or drop off, the mail. For a while ships called in at Kingswear for passengers traffic and mail on the New York run, to the Middle East and to South Africa. The scene must have been one of great activity and movement, all swathed in clouds of steam from railway engines, cranes and ships alike. There were also those specific upheavals of Empire such as during the Zulu Wars in South Africa. One such moment was on 26 February 1879 when the *Dublin Castle*, out of London with 700 men and 32 officers of the 60th Rifles, set sail for the Cape. She had called in to coal and take on last-minute provisions, including mail and livestock! Trainloads of locals from Exeter and Torbay arrived to wave the soldiers off with bands playing and flags flying and no doubt a tear or two.

However, in the commercial race of port development, Southampton, with its closer proximity to London and far greater expanse of water, was to win in the end. No doubt the shareholders of the Dartmouth & Torbay Railway Company were disappointed men, but for later generations the majority have heaved a sigh of relief at this particular failure.

Having followed the footpath through Hoodown and over Waterhead Creek viaduct, you cross the railway by means of the railway footbridge and climb up on to Belgravia and the modern piece of road engineering known as the Banjo. Before walking down to the passenger ferry take one last look over the wall at Waterhead Creek. Think back to its early days as a shipyard, then buried under the industrial revolution of railway sidings and turntable, in its turn eradicated by the modern requirements of maritime recreation and the motor car. What next I wonder?

Turn in under the archway that separates the station from the Royal Dart Hotel and add your footsteps to those who alighted from the London train to take

Left and below: *The evocative scenes of sail and steam that have provided movement and sound in and around the waters of Kingswear for the past 150 years.*

their place on the railway ferry across the river. In 1869 a special railway ferry, *Dolphin*, was commissioned to take railway passengers on the final leg of their journey to Dartmouth. Way back in 1858 Dartmouth had been prescribed as the destination of this railway, even though the line itself was not to be. The reason for this will be made apparent in the next chapter. Dartmouth became the only railway station in the country that has never seen a train.

The days of GWR's two great floating pontoons, with their canopies of corrugated iron sheeting, rising and falling on the tide, are long gone. Today River Link continues its service to locals and holidaymakers alike, providing the third link in the chain across the river.

*The ferry across to Dartmouth Station, the only railway station in Britain never to welcome a train!*

Chapter 6

# *Dart Valley Trail*

The time has come to leave the port of Dartmouth and its communities either side of the river. This circular walk of 8 miles can be started from a variety of points.
1. Dartmouth Central Car park, off Mayor's Avenue.
2. Dartside Marina Car park, Kingswear.
3. Greenway Quay, Greenway.
4. Dittisham Car park, The Level, Dittisham.

For the purposes of this chapter we will take Dartmouth as our starting and finishing point.

Initially, you will be covering some familiar territory, taking either the River Link Passenger Ferry from beside the old station building, or the Lower Car Ferry, the successor of the 'Horse Ferry'. Once in Kingswear walk up Fore Street to its junction with the railway footbridge and make your way down to the footpath running between the railway track and the river. Follow the path for a couple of hundred yards until you arrive at a gate and pedestrian crossing over the railway track. An interesting observation in the estuary, should the tide be out, is regular lines of small objects dotted across the mud flats. Usually these comprise pieces of fragmented pipe-work, positioned to stimulate peeler crab populating the river bed in readiness for the anglers who find them a very successful bait. Crossing the track with great care, a path will lead you up through the sessile oaks of Hoodown Wood. After a climb of approximately 150 feet you will join a path contouring the side of the valley where you need to bear to the left.

This is your first immersion into the oakwoods of the Dart valley that provide such a characteristic mantle from water's edge to skyline. The National Trust

*The railway seemingly plunges into the oak-swathed hillside of the Dart.*

now own and manage 32 acres of Hoodown Wood, the first of a number of parcels of woodland along the valley side.

After a couple of hundred yards, with glimpses of estuary below to your left, an area of meadow will come into view on your right. For a brief three-year period, from 1934–37, this was part of Kingswear's 18-hole golf course. The Golf House still remains, now as a private residence, and our route will soon join with the access drive to it. Continue along the semi-metalled roadway until you abruptly join the higher ferry road from Hillhead. Your route requires that you cross the road here to the path access just down hill. It is very much a blind corner and great care needs to be taken in listening out for approaching traffic, especially when the ferry has just come in.

The path plunges you immediately down a flight of steps into Noss Wood and a spacious natural environment of luxuriant ferns and fauna set beneath a high woodland canopy. It is so tucked away that hardly a whisper of a breeze is felt here and if woodland spirits exist anywhere this is where you will meet them.

This magic area is now abruptly terminated by a private road leading down to Noss Marina, once Philip & Son shipyard. More of this from a better vantage point to come. Your path continues from the far side of the private road, 50 yards up hill. However, the magic dell is now replaced by denser undergrowth and woodland growth as the path turns to follow the line of Noss Creek away from the estuary for half a mile. High up above the creek on the north ridge of the valley is cut one of those ancient forts of the Iron Age. Noticeable today by its distinct circular fringe of trees this defensive enclosure provided sanctuary for the dispersed farming folk in times of threat some 2500 to 2000 years ago.

*The charcoal cutters' track contours through Long Wood with the river glimpsed below.*

Having crossed the Noss stream, the track now returns towards the estuary, climbing up the valley side to provide a panoramic view of the river as you enter Long Wood. The National Trust took over the stewardship of 101 acres of Long Wood, together with adjacent areas of Noss Plantation and Cart Wood, in 1981. It is due to the Trust that the track you are walking on, often referred to as the charcoal cutters' track, is now accessible to the public. For centuries the oak was utilized as a vital natural product of the land, from this woodland and every other bounding the river estuary. Carefully selected stands were cut, seasoned and taken to the nearby shipyards at Dartmouth, Kingswear, Galmpton and Brixham to provide keels, knees and frames for trading, fishing and naval vessels alike. Less suitable trees were coppiced to provide the raw material for charcoal production, a fuel indispensable in earlier days for the smithy's furnace and for firing the local lime kilns.

Below you, looking downstream you can see the old shipyard of Philip & Son, still recognisable as such, although its status is now that of a marina and all shipbuilding and repair work have ceased. It started life back in 1891 under the inspired partnership of Simpson Strickland. Francis Simpson who was so averse to the building of the South Embankment, helped create a major source of employment for the Dartmouth area for the next hundred years. Their yard was state-of-the-art for its time and here they designed and built, in timber and steel and lead, steam yachts for the well-heeled of society. In 1883 Simpson purchased land further upriver at the base of the Greenway peninsula. Here he built a fine mansion, Maypool House, that you will be able to study more closely as you progress along the route. The position of the house provided admirable views of the estuary, and his boatyard. It is said a powerful telescope was situated at the house for Simpson to keep an eye on his workers!

*The old shipyard of Philip & Son, now sadly deceased, often simply referred to as Noss.*

The First World War brought considerable work from the Admiralty but also, alas, bankruptcy for Simpson Strickland who were forced to sell their yard to Philip & Son in 1918. Under Philips, Noss and Sandquay yards became a major shipbuilding centre for the South West. Amongst other customers Trinity House used Philips to build lightships, and in 1923 twenty-three vessels of various type where constructed here. Skilled workers came to Philip's yard from towns and villages such as Brixham and Dittisham as well as Dartmouth. Apprenticeships where highly prized and a three-mile walk to work from Brixham was a price well worth paying. For Dartmouth and Dittisham men and boys the river provided an easier form of transportation.

Also in 1923 the strangulation of the yard by the railway was finally overcome. From its construction the line was carried over the entrance to Noss Creek on two sections of wooden viaduct under which vessels from the yard had to pass in order to gain access to the river. With the yard becoming busier and vessels larger, the situation became intolerable. So in 1923 a 'deviation' of the line was engineered to take the line in a curve behind the shipyard. With the viaducts demolished the yard then had unencumbered access to the estuary.

The Second World War saw Philip & Son employing 500 workers, all busily engaged in constructing 230 vessels for the Admiralty, mainly small craft such as corvettes, minesweepers, MTBs and MGBs. During September 1942 a German hit-and-run raid caused great loss of life, considerable damage and a brief disruption to the war effort. Twenty men were killed and forty injured, the worst casualties inflicted on the immediate Dartmouth area throughout the war.

Following the war, Philips continued to provide employment on both sides of the river until the 1960s when it sold Noss to Reeves & Co, timber merchants of Totnes. This company introduced marina services to the yard, the beginning of the end as far as boat construction and repair was concerned. However, there was one last attempt to breathe life into the yard and the port of Dartmouth as a whole. In 1987 outline plans were drawn up for a three-berth dock capable of taking ships up to 10 000 tons. Costing £7 million for construction and additional infrastructure the plan was to resurrect Dartmouth as a commercial port, a second coming of the railways! This was not to be. Twentieth-century concepts of conservation, recreational demands and an intense protectionism by locals of all social stratas saw the scheme aborted.

Before moving on your way from this idyllic vantage point it is worth a moment to identify features on the far side of the valley that will bear a closer relationship to your walk in its latter stages. Down stream is Old Mill Creek, running away in a cleavage between the hills, with the grounds of Britannia Royal Naval College rising up on its southern flank. This largely unclaimed creek gives us some idea of what Dartmouth's coombe, now reclaimed, would have resembled before man's intervention. Immediately opposite, right down on the water's edge, is Lower Kilngate. Accessible by river or from Bozomzeal, high above, Lower Kilngate was once a small farmstead. Legend has it that in the time of the *Mayflower* and *Speedwell*'s visit in 1620, the farmer was sympathetic to the Puritan cause and invited the emigrants to a prayer meeting away from the prying eyes of the town and the local ecclesiastical establishment.

Having had your fill, the charcoal cutters' track takes you along the hillside with the river below and, given the correct seasons of the year, winter and springtime, intermittent views of distant Greenway and Dittisham through the bare or budding branches. Early summer is introduced with a blanket of bluebells and one knows the summer season has arrived when the sound and nostalgic smell of steam trains make their presence felt on the railway line running parallel with the charcoal cutters' track and the river below.

Eventually the route of the track will require a burst of energy as it turns to climb quite steeply up the hillside, firstly up a steady gradient and then a flight of irregular steps cut into the hillside. Now a path once more, your route levels out at around 250 feet above the river and exits Long Wood and National Trust land at a stile to continue on through Oakum Woods towards Higher Greenway and Maypool. Oakum was a fibrous material produced from old rope to caulk (fill) the spaces between ships' planking thus stopping leaking. It was often produced (or picked) by inmates of workhouses and prisons and was an incredibly arduous job, but very necessary in the construction of wooden ships. Although locally relevant there is no known association of Oakum wood with this particular trade, other than by name.

Once in Oakum Woods keep an eye out to your left, through the trees and a vantage point will provide you with a view of Simpson's Maypool House across a deep, tree-filled bowl adjacent to the estuary. The footpath will gently take you down around the perimeter of this natural indentation to the outbuildings of what was once Higher Greenway Farm. Once part of Lord

Churston's estate, the farm buildings have recently been largely converted into residential accommodation but still sit comfortably on the summit of a ridge overlooking the estuary and Maypool.

Where the farm track meets the tarmac lane turn left. For a brief stretch the way now follows an extremely ancient overland route, both from nearby Galmpton village to Greenway, but also from Churston Cove, near Brixham to Greenway, and thence across the river to Dittisham and on overland to Halwell and Stanborough, the ancient administrative centre of the South Hams in pre-Saxon times.

The name Maypool relates primarily to the freshwater pool down in the valley below. It is thought that the pool originated from the extraction of marl (clay), the pit then flooding to provide a freshwater pool, three acres in extent, which then became an ideal habitat for perch and eels. This feature is best viewed from the river itself but you will also gain a glimpse of it once the river has been crossed and you are climbing the western valley slopes above Dittisham. Immediately behind the pool stands the dominant structure of the Maypool viaduct, built in 1862–63 of local limestone, ninety feet above the valley floor to carry the railway along its route through Long Wood to the entrance of Greenway tunnel. More of the relevance and influence of this dual engineering feat a little later.

*Maypool Viaduct introduces the railway line to Long Wood and its distant destination of Kingswear and Dartmouth.*

The surrounding area of the pool and a variety of buildings are also identified as Maypool. During the latter days of the Newfoundland cod trade the boathouse, situated on the water frontage, was used to store the valuable train oil (cod liver oil). Above the pool Maypool House remains as the dominant residence. When Francis Simpson built the house in 1883 the surrounding buildings, including the pool and boathouse, were all part of his estate. Buildings adjacent to the house, now private residences, were originally used as staff accommodation, stabling and garaging. Built predominantly of local red sandstone and limestone this elegant pile provided a residence for members of the Simpson family until well after the First World War. In 1912 Mrs Simpson was to be one of the last members of the family at Maypool to follow an ancient tradition of the estuary when her body was taken down river from Greenway Quay for burial at St Clement, Townstal.

*Maypool Boathouse, now converted into a residence but once thought to have been used for the storage of train oil, a product of the Newfoundland cod fishery.*

As you pass the entrance to Maypool House, now well utilised as a superbly positioned Youth Hostel, the road gives way to a track once more, a very ancient track. The back of the house can be glimpsed through the trees. In fact legend has it that on certain nights, past residents of Maypool House were aware of the sound of coach wheels and clattering hooves – and yet there was nothing to be seen.

Once past Maypool House the track brings you to the boundary of the Greenway Estate, now the property of the National Trust. This estate, now totalling 280 acres, was given to the Trust in 2000 by the Hicks family. The outlying estate, which includes a network of footpaths is accessible to you throughout the year.

You enter Greenway along the line of the old routeway as it gently descends towards the Quay. However your progress along it is to be brief, but exquisite, as the view of the estuary with Dartmouth in the distance unfolds from your vantage point on the upper slopes of a grassy meadow, 250 feet above the river. This is the first, and certainly not the last, experience that Greenway is to provide where time is needed to contemplate the sheer magnificence of a natural scene, whatever the season of the year. When you feel able to tear yourself away it will simply be to move on to the next visual treat. The right-of-way now turns right, up on to the apex of the Greenway ridge where a vista of 180 degrees of estuary provides you with nearly the entire run of the tidal reach, from Dartmouth to the isolated pile of Sharpham and the distant ridges of Dartmoor. Facing west, to your front is the village of Dittisham with a section of the intervening river hidden by the lie of the land and its woodland covering. Also well hidden from this 300 foot vantage point are Greenway House and its surrounding gardens. The topography of the area is clear to see with Greenway a promontory, surrounded by the river on three sides. Geology has defined the course of the river, confined by hard volcanic rocks, to cut and create the great meander on either side of which Greenway and Dittisham have developed.

As you begin to descend the upriver slope from the ridge you will pass through an old Victorian wrought-iron kissing gate (ignore the right-of-way leading off to your right) before dropping steeply across the meadow to the car park of Greenway Gardens. Here your choice of action will depend on the season and day of the week. Your route, as far as this chapter is concerned, is to take you on down directly to Greenway Quay, a route that is always available to you. From March until October Greenway Garden is open to visitors four days a week. As Greenway has played such a pivotal role in the history of the estuary, county and country, aspects of its development are a very necessary ingredient of this book and therefore the subject specifically dealt with in the following chapter.

Continuing your way along the Dart Valley Trail, exit the Greenway Gardens car park and turn right up the drive towards Carlyon's Lodge. On joining the

*Looking south from the hillside pastures of the Greenway estate to the Port of Dartmouth.*

*Looking north, upstream towards Sharpham House and the distant hills of Dartmoor.*

highway, turn left and make your way down to Greenway Quay. On your way you cannot miss the majestic silver-grey stands of beech that dominate your path, whatever the season. Keep an eye out though, on your right, set between the road and the river for the old laundry house, now Hunter's Moon, a private residence. Built by Richard Harvey this once very utilitarian building was where the laundry work for Greenway House was carried out. You will notice the narrow drive going off to your left that originally joined house to laundry.

Greenway Quay together with its associated ferryman's cottage is another of the Dart's gems, this time providing a vantage point from river level. Many a weathered sailor of worldly experience has qualified these waters as the most beautiful anchorage on Earth and it is likely that Queen Victoria's statement that likened the estuary to 'the English Rhine' was stimulated as she sailed through these narrows with the heights rising up on either side. The crossing is 250 yards in width, these days for foot passengers and cyclists only. The days of the horse-ferry transporting livestock on their way to Galmpton market are long gone, as interestingly is the car ferry that had a brief existence. The bell and its ringing chime still rings out however to summon the ferryman. Make the most of your landing on the Dittisham pontoon as this will provide you with your last few paces of level walking for a while before starting your ascent up Manor Street.

Above: *Greenway Quay and its associated ferryman's cottage.*

Right: *The landing jetty and pontoon at Dittisham complete with its attendant, multicoloured craft.*

Dittisham (pronounced Ditsum by many locals) is a village that has grown from the river and its surrounding rural landscape. Today it has become a retreat for those lucky enough to afford excessive property values, protected from the excesses of present-day Torbay by the river. This particular walk will introduce you to the southern part only of what is intrinsically a linear village, identified as lower Dittisham, with further exploration of higher Dittisham in Chapter 10. The walk up Manor Street should be made at a comfortable stroll in order to enjoy the varying cottages with their descriptive identities – Fisherman's Cottage, The Cider, Fern Cottage, the Old Bake House, Plum Tree Cottage being but a few. As well as salmon fishing, Dittisham has been famous for its Ploughman Plums ever since the original young trees arrived here, courtesy of a German shipwreck. Autumn has been characterised by the placing of baskets of fruit outside the cottages with the relevant dish for your dues, with dishonesty or theft simply not considered a problem. For generations the men of Dittisham travelled the seas as both crew and master on the ships of Dartmouth. There were also those who went off to find a fortune in the Californian gold fields of the 1850s – and some succeeded and returned to their native village as wealthy men. At the top of Manor Street and its junction with The Level, the elegant residence Otago is the result of one such enterprise.

Above: *Manor Street, with its variety of well-preserved cottages leads down to the water's edge and the ferry.*

Left: *Smugglers Cottage sits aloof on its tidal quay.*

*Picturesque Dittisham Quay where, during the season, motor vehicles are now found where salmon skiffs were once pulled up on the firm foreshore.*

At this point your route turns left into Rectory Lane, leading you out of the village in a southerly direction and then, following the way-marks, on up the hillside along a farm track for a further 250 yards. Now, a turn to your left, another stile and a curving climb on up over the hillside with the Dart estuary opening up once again below in what is considered to be one of the most beautiful views in Devon. Immediately below is the roof-top of the Old Dittisham Rectory. Georgian in age, it provided successive Rectors with a suitable residence as Lords of the Manor of Dittisham, a title bequeathed since 1632. Beyond lies the tree-covered Greenway promontory with its house peeking out from within its green mantle. In the distance lie the waters of Torbay, whilst closer is a great crescent of tidal estuary known as Broad Reach or Dittisham Lake. This is the largest area of open water on the estuary and is marked by a curving sand and mud bank known as Flat Owers, plainly visible at low water but a navigational black-spot to the unwary sailor on a falling tide. Was this expanse of sheltered water the nursery training ground for the sailors of Raleigh and the Gilberts as it is for the young sailors of today? Highly likely.

Your climb continues on up across the fields until the summit and a quiet country lane is reached, over 500 feet (160m) above the river at Dittisham. Quite some achievement but well worth the effort! Having turned left along

*A panoramic vista of Broad Reach and Greenway with the waters of nearby Torbay providing the backdrop.*

the lane you will soon have to decide whether you wish to continue along the more direct route towards Dartmouth, or to turn off to your left and take a slightly longer loop which will take you closer to the river and along the northern slopes of Old Mill Creek. Visible from either route you will see the Fire Beacon, resurrected in 1988 to commemorate the defeat of the Armada, appropriate in that the majority of the land between Dittisham and Old Mill Creek remains part of the Raleigh Estate.

*The Beacon crowning the summit.*

One advantage of staying on the direct route is that you then soon pass the tiny hamlet and Manor House of Bozomzeal to your left. Of Saxon origin, it once belonging to Gytha, mother of King Harold, later becoming a monastic holding. The present Manor House still includes a Great Hall complete with medieval fireplace and the remains of a Norman arch. Set in an indentation below the hillside summit, its isolated rural setting can still be identified with its Saxon origins.

Soon your route leaves the lane, turning off to the right. Following a bird's-eye view of the port of Dartmouth, with the use of footpath and track, you now make an enthralling descent through combe and woodland towards the head of Old Mill Creek. You will notice this creek is very much a work-

shop set amongst the trees. No plush, immaculate marina here but a place where the river boats are serviced and repaired in readiness for the forthcoming season.

The old mill is easily recognised as you cross the bridge and creek. It is worth a pause here, a seat on the parapet of the bridge to gather yourself in preparation for the steep (and it is steep) climb up 400 feet to Townstal along Old Mill Lane. You will be ready to lean on that very appropriate gate two-thirds of the way up to regain your breath and enjoy the view of the river adjacent to Philips Marina and, in the distance, that circular doughnut of trees on the hillside that marks out the ancient Iron Age hill fort of Noss. Follow the lane, through the housing estate to its junction with the main road. Cross the road into Church Road and here you enter the heart of the old village.

Above: *The spars and galvanized-iron roofs of Old Mill Creek and its associated boat-repair yards.*

Right: *The old mill.*

Below: *View from a gate: Noss yard and the Iron Age camp.*

Your exertions required in climbing the heights help qualify the suitability of this site, high up on the ridge, when the Saxons arrived and were looking for a safe situation, away from prying Viking eyes. The Saxon Manor of Townstal (Tunstal) was one of a series of manors closely associated with each other. At one time it is highly likely that Townstal was an integral part of the Manor of

Stoke Fleming. William the Conqueror's Domesday confirms for us that Townstal consisted of four smallholders, five villagers and two slaves. They possessed six cattle, forty sheep and fifteen goats and ploughed what little land was suitable with two plough teams. Domesday also confirms that no such place as Dartmouth existed – here was the birthplace of what was to become a thriving port, 400 feet up the hill. Today the site of that original settlement is well defined by Dartmouth's mother church of St Clement and the Old Farmhouse, now a picturesque hotel, relating well to Townstal's rural roots. Townstal's character was to change dramatically, starting between the wars. This was the provision of new housing for those living in slum conditions in the older part of the town. These slums had very often been the homes of the 'lumpers' and their families, the men who had been responsible for coaling the ships during the years when Dartmouth was such an important coaling port. Today Townstal continues to be the main area for providing affordable housing for the working population of the town.

*The Church of St Clement, heart of the Saxon settlement of Tunstal, the seed from which the town of Dartmouth would blossom.*

Your route will now make one final descent into Dartmouth town where we continue, if possible, to follow the ancient routes used long before the days of the internal combustion engine. Continue on down Church Road, crossing over Victoria Road into Mount Boone. One hundred yards down Mount Boone, bear right down Townstal Hill and thence into the narrows of Clarence Hill. You will now descend into the bosom of the maritime town, leaving noise and exhaust fumes behind. Keep an eye open because you then need to turn to your right, down Clarence Steps, the way of the horse trains of old, bringing their pannier loads down to market. Your arrival at the base of the steps brings you out at the northern end of Foss Street, under Hardness – you have come full-circle – your journey is complete.

*Clarence Steps, one of the ancient routes into Dartmouth, down which the pannier-laden ponies would descend.*

Chapter 7

# *Greenway – Historic Secret Garden of the Dart*

The narrows at Greenway have been a crossing place of the river for thousands of years. Those who make their way across on the ferry will be following in the watery footsteps of our Bronze and Iron Age ancestors. The first major dwelling associated with the name of Greenway was only to come into being during the sixteenth century, in the reign of Henry VIII. It was here that Otho Gilbert, son of Otho of Compton, would build a new home, Greenway Court, for his young bride Katherine (née Champernowne of Modbury) in c.1530. It is thought that this original house stood somewhere in the area of the present National Trust reception area and adjacent tennis court.

*An early nineteenth century illustration of Greenway by William Payne in which both original sixteenth-century Court and later Regency mansion are included.*

Katherine provided Otho with three sons, John, Humphrey and Adrian. Otho died in 1547 and Katherine soon remarried into the Raleighs* of Fardel in East Devon. John became the Master of Greenway upon his mother's move to Hayes Barton, followed by the birth of three further children, one to become Sir Walter Raleigh. It was the union of Champernownes, Gilberts and Raleighs that was one of the major driving forces in the expansionist period of Tudor and Stuart England, especially in the direction of the Americas. Their position was greatly enhanced due to the fact that both Sir Humphrey Gilbert and Sir Walter Raleigh became great favourites of Queen Elizabeth and wielded great influence and power.

There is no doubt that Greenway Court must have become one of the centres of planning for some of the great expeditions of the era, and it was Sir Humphrey, soldier, explorer and merchant adventurer, whose persistence and determination would finally be rewarded by the Queen when she provided him with Letters Patent, official approval to seek out new lands in her name. The objective and driving force of nearly every expedition was financial profit.

*Greenway Boathouse, but also importantly, a bathing house, complete with pool.*

* Modern historians take the spelling of the family name as Ralegh. The author has preferred to adopt the spelling used by many, including his illustrious historian forebear, Tristram Risdon.

Above: *Sir Humphrey Gilbert of Compton.*
(by kind permission of Geoffrey Gilbert)

Below: *The Anchor Stone or Scold Stone, as seen from Greenway Garden.*

The lure of Cathay and a means to bypass the stranglehold of Spain and Portugal by finding a North West Passage around the Americas, Spanish gold, and some privateering as a side-line – all provided an incentive. Initially approved in 1578, Sir Humphrey's first efforts were a failure. Interestingly one of the ships of this first expedition was the *Hope of Greenway* commanded by Sir Walter's brother, Carew Raleigh. However, in 1583 Sir Humphrey found success with the planting of the flag on the 'New-found-land', and England had its first possession on the far side of the Atlantic. This time the reward followed, not in the form of gold but of cod from off its shores. Sadly, on the return voyage the two ships remaining experienced a severe storm and Sir Humphrey's ship *Squirrel* foundered with all hands lost. However, Sir Humphrey Gilbert of Greenway and Compton was remembered as the man whose exploits gave breath to an embryonic empire, the forerunner of the British Empire.

Following Sir Humphrey's death the 'initiative' was continued by the other members of the family. During 1884 Adrian Gilbert, together with John Davis of Sandridge (more of this gentleman in a later chapter), were given authorisation to seek out a North West Passage, whilst Sir Walter Raleigh was provided with the Letters Patent of the late Sir Humphrey, further accreditation of his power and influence at this time, and his near fanatical interest in the colonisation of Virginia of which he became Governor for a while.

During the height of his popularity with the Queen he also held the positions of Captain of the Queen's Guard, Lord Warden of the Stannaries, Lord Lieutenant of Cornwall and Vice Admiral of Cornwall and Devon with his half-brother, Sir John Gilbert, being Vice Admiral of Devon. Although a rare visitor to the Dart, his influence and support locally was immense, even following his fall from grace towards the end of Elizabeth's reign. The boat house at Greenway is often referred to as Raleigh's boat house (only one small section of the building actually being a boat house) and although the present building shows no resemblance to its Tudor structure it is more than likely that a boat house was here to provide transportation between Greenway Court and the wharves and ships downriver at Dartmouth and Kingswear. Land on the far side of the river still falls under the title of the Raleigh Estates and local legend has it that Sir Walter's first pipe of Virginia tobacco was smoked on English soil hereabouts, even on the Anchor Stone, if you are to believe the commentaries of the passing river boats. The Anchor Stone, or 'Scold Stone' as it is sometimes known, has close associations with the nearby community of Dittisham, although it is best seen, either from a boat or from the battery within Greenway

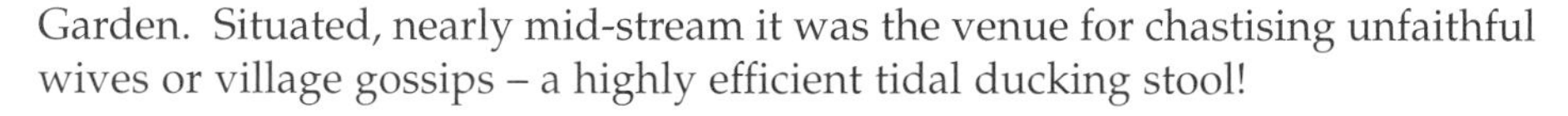

Garden. Situated, nearly mid-stream it was the venue for chastising unfaithful wives or village gossips – a highly efficient tidal ducking stool!

The peaceful view from Greenway boathouse takes in the Tudor dwellings of Hamlyn's Coombe, once the property of Raleigh and said to have been one of his hunting lodges. Hunting has certainly been a popular pastime for this area of the Dart over the centuries and Britannia Royal Naval College, having been built on the Raleigh Estates, continued the tradition by running a pack of beagles which is still retained to this day.

The year 1588 saw the arrival of the Spanish Armada off England's shores and not unexpectedly the Gilberts and Raleigh were involved both directly and indirectly. Sir John and Adrian Gilbert provided three ships from Dartmouth for the defence of the country. It was one of Raleigh's ships, the *Roebuck,* which escorted the captured Spanish galleon *Nuestra Senora del Rosario* into Torbay where her soldiers were taken off and imprisoned in the tithe barn of

Above left: *The Battery, thought to have been constructed in Napoleonic times to deter French incursions upriver.*

Above: *The Camellia Garden, providing an explosion of springtime blossom.*

Torre Abbey, now known as the Spanish Barn. The ship was then brought round to Dartmouth where Sir John, as Vice Admiral of Devon, was made responsible for ship, contents and crew. Much to the consternation of his fellow Vice Admiral, George Cary of Cockington, Sir John took advantage of his position and set his prisoners to work at Greenway. History records '106 of the said Spanish prisoners remaining a-ship board hard by his house at Greenway to every day hardly labour in his garden in the levelling of his grounds'. The first mention of garden landscaping at Greenway!

*Greenway House.*

The name Raleigh Gilbert lives on today at Compton Castle, a fitting continuity of family and links of the West Country with the Americas. The close ties of family and trade continued in strength throughout the sixteenth and seventeenth centuries for many communities associated with the Dart. For Greenway also, the new master in the 1780s, Roope Harris Roope, had close ties with both nearby Dittisham and New England. Roope's grandfather originated from Dittisham from where he emigrated to New England and became a successful merchant trader. Roope continued the family business from Greenway, very much involved in the Newfoundland cod trade, with trading links in Spain, Portugal and Virginia. His marriage to Mary was a highly productive one providing them with a family of fifteen children! Although not totally proven it is thought that Roope was the builder of the Regency period Greenway House – to provide greater living space for the expanding family no doubt. Certainly the new house had been constructed by 1791 when Edward Elton purchased Greenway.

Edward's son, James Marwood Elton took over Greenway in 1811 following the death of his father. He added two further wings to the new house, possibly to provide the appropriate status necessary for a High Sheriff of Devon. It was during his ownership that changes were made to road access from the village of Galmpton to the ferry, allowing the new drive to be constructed along its present route.

It was also somewhere around the turn of the eighteenth and nineteenth centuries that the bathing house, attached to the boathouse, was first constructed. Following the famed event of King George III emersing his royal body in the sea at Weymouth in 1789, 'taking the waters' for the good of your health became an important social event for the aristocracy and gentry of Britain. With nearby Torquay becoming an exclusive watering place the increased status of Greenway having its own watering facilities must have been considerable. Seawater was the required raw-material and the tide provided a constant supply to combat the dreaded consumption and other pulmonary illnesses.

James sold Greenway in 1832 and so began a century of major influence by the landed gentry of Cornwall. Firstly the Carlyons of Tregrehan who added the

*The early nineteenth-century main drive, added by James Marwood Elton.*

*The subtlety of the semi-wild garden set within the wooded slopes of the Dart estuary provides an environment of peace, totally at ease with itself.*

Lodge to the drive entrance in 1850, and the beeches along its length. Following a brief interlude, Richard Harvey of Gwennap purchased Greenway and the Manorial holding of Galmpton using his fortune gained from tin and copper mining. The Harvey years had a radical effect on the entire area, the influence of which remains today. As squire he modernised the village, his wife Susanna later adding the village school in memory of her husband. But Richard's aversion to the new-fangled railway was to have the greatest long-term effect on not just Greenway but the estuary, Dartmouth and the South Hams of today. The original plan of the Dartmouth & Torbay Railway Company was to take the railway down to Greenway Quay, then on by ferry, with an option to later bridge the Dart here and hence take the line on down to Dartmouth. Richard took his objections to the House of Lords and in March 1861 the railway company was forced to realign the route through a mutually agreed tunnel under Harvey land and on down through Long Wood to Kingswear. Richard Harvey was the man responsible for Dartmouth having a railway station with no railway line but more importantly, for having an estuary unbridged to Totnes. Should the railway have gained their bridge, road bridges would surely have followed, with the subsequent effect on development.

Following Susanna's death in 1882, Thomas Bolitho of Trewidden, banker and smelter, purchased Greenway and the Manor of Galmpton and continued the work of his predecessors. His daughter Mary was then to retain Greenway as her home when she married Charles Williams, again of Cornish influence, initially MP for Tavistock and then Torquay. In 1937 they sold Greenway independently from the rest of the estate and a year later Mr and Mrs Max Mallowan took over ownership of their 32 acres of Greenway. Agatha Christie had arrived.

*The clean lines of the stable yard with neatly laid granite sets. Today this provides the National Trust with its reception area for the garden visitor.*

The war intervened briefly in the Mallowan's plans for Greenway. For a time it was used as a residence for evacuees before being requisitioned by the Admiralty in 1943 for use as an Officers' Mess for the US Navy 10th Patrol Boat Squadron. Once again Greenway was linked with the Americas and seemingly the Mallowans were sympathetic to historic ties in that the artistic interpretation of naval actions participated in by the 10th Flotilla, painted on the frieze around the library by Lt. Marshall Lee, were requested to be left intact and not painted over when the time came for the US Navy to leave. In 1946 Greenway was returned to Agatha and her husband where it became their retreat and summer home in Devon for the latter years of their lives. There must have been times when her surroundings here stimulated that creative mind to another plot, such as took place in the bathhouse when in *Dead Man's Folly* Marlene Tucker is found strangled on the salon floor. A fictional foul deed set amongst tranquil and peaceful surroundings.

*Early autumnal light illuminates a peaceful river.*

Mrs M, as she was known by locals associated with Greenway, continued the common denominator characterised by the majority of Greenway's owners over 500 years – the love and nurturing of trees and plants in this most perfect of settings. Each owner in turn has added his or her own individuality, often in such subtle ways that they appear as fascinating surprises in this secret garden on the Dart. In 1959 Agatha's daughter, Rosalind Hicks bought Greenway from her mother and has lived here with her husband since 1967, adding to and identifying with the character that is Greenway.

One remaining addition to Greenway's natural beauty and unique history is its wildlife. Always present in one form or another but best seen in one of those more tranquil moments. The garden includes a heronry situated high up in Scots pines between the boathouses of Greenway and Maypool. Its inhabitants can often be seen feeding in the shallows as the tide recedes or encroaches over Parson's Mud on the western shore. Now also the herons have the increasing company of white egrets and, of course the ever-present cormorants. For the sharp-eyed there is the darting flash of kingfisher and then if you are lucky the curious gaze of a grey seal that calls the estuary its home. For a chance to glimpse one or more of these lovely creatures the quay adjoining Greenway bathing house, or the battery, make perfect stations, for those who have time to wait, ponder and watch.

Chapter 8

# *Galmpton Creek – Site of Industrial Heritage*

The route of this circular walk epitomises the broad spectrum of the Dart as a working environment for generations of working men and their families, set in a scenic wonderland. One is fascinated by the thought – how many had the time and inclination to appreciate this landscape during their daily toil as many of the present generation do today? Our route will in fact take in the terrain on either side of Galmpton Creek, together with a further appraisal of the Greenway promontory for the return leg to Galmpton which will provide further stunning views of the river.

The recommended starting point for this exploration is Galmpton Post Office and Stores (SX886563), or the Manor Inn, a couple of hundred yards up the road. The village of Galmpton lies in a shallow valley within the Dart catchment but set back and barely visible from the river. Its rural Saxon origins provided its identity and continuity right up to the 1940s with the land its mainstay, and apple orchards and individually owned piggeries providing important staples for the village community. For many generations the Lords of the Manor, then Squires of Galmpton, resided at Greenway and therefore the bond between village and estate has been strong, with the Harveys and then the Bolithos very much associated with the modernisation of the village during late Victorian and Edwardian times. However, the river has also played an immensely important part in the history of the community as you will see as you progress; hardly surprising considering the length of the parish boundary which comprises river frontage.

Follow the Stoke Gabriel Road down through the village. At the junction of this road with Kiln Road just pause a moment to take in the view of Manor Farmhouse to your left and the redeveloped farm buildings of Manor Court opposite. This farm was once one of the Greenway Estate tenant farms with its land extending right down to the river and Galmpton Creek. The nineteenth century buildings are constructed of local Devonian limestone on which this area rests. Once past the farm building, Kiln Road leads into an area that has been extensively quarried over the past couple of centuries, before reaching the creek. The reference to a kiln also provides the clue to another by-product of the limestone – lime. We will return to this in more detail later but for now continue your journey along the country lane of the Stoke Gabriel Road and on up the steep, twisting rise of Port Hill. A last glimpse back over the hedgerow will help you appreciate how well Galmpton is tucked away in its little valley.

On reaching the brow of the hill a further hundred yards will bring you to a stile on the left-hand side of the road. The hedgerow leading away from the stile is pointing you in the direction of your route and was also the old parish boundary of Churston and Galmpton. Having crossed two fields, you will enter the third to be greeted by a superb panoramic view of Galmpton Creek, the Greenway promontory beyond, the waters of Broad Reach and distant

*Broad Reach – difficult to believe that the waters of the Dart flow out between the Greenway promontory and Dittisham. With low water approaching the curving muddy expanse of Flat Owers makes an appearance once more.*

Dittisham. Such a view inspires one to give thanks for the preservation of the landscape and the determination of Richard Harvey in obstructing the building of a bridge. It should also awaken us to our responsibilities for the future management of such sites and the real relevance and importance of the National Trust in acting as guardians.

It is difficult to appreciate from this point but the land on either side of the field down which you descend was once occupied by great quarries, now partially softened by nature and then utilised by present-day commercial activities largely associated with the marine world. What a fine line of historical development, luck and judgement has been drawn when one compares the two very different landscapes lying so closely together.

Clambering down over a stile at the bottom left-hand corner of the field you enter Galmpton Boatyard, set within the masked cliffs of redundant quarry workings. The first recorded ship to be built here was the 38-ton *Sarah*, registered 1834. The original yard was run by William Gibbs and, during the next hundred years, numerous trading vessels, steam yachts and Brixham fishing smacks were built of timber, iron or steel. The construction of Brixham sailing trawlers was a major initiative at the Galmpton yard, with 250 craft being built. Many were destined for owners in sea ports around the country where the skills and craftsmanship of the local yard were renowned. Three such craft, *Leader*, *Provident* and *Golden Vanity*, built at Galmpton, can be seen today, sailing out of Brixham as part of the town's Heritage Fleet.

*Galmpton Boatyard as it was back in the 1970s. The remains of the old Sandquay are still visible in the foreground.*

In 1906 the name of Gibbs was superseded by Sanders & Co and work gradually transferred from building to repair. Amongst the work carried out between the wars was the refitting of majestic J-Class yachts, which in those days were able to navigate the approaches to the yard due to dredging. Today the boat-repair business has experienced a considerable increase in trade locally with many skills represented. The redundant quarry floors have made excellent storage areas for leisure craft and working boats, and where limestone was once loaded into vessels, craft of all shapes and sizes are lifted out for wintering or repair.

As you exit the yard bear slightly right into the car park area and note the remains of an old weighbridge set into the ground. This structure, together with a short section of railway line along the quayside, were positioned here in the 1930s when river sand was landed here, washed and taken out by lorry.

This superseded the longer journey that the sailing ketches *Effort* and *Mizpah* used to make round to the Corporation's North Quay at Torquay harbour. Both vessels used to dredge the sand from the bottom of the river using a canvas bag, the best quality sand coming from the stretch of the river between Stoke Gabriel and Sharpham. It was described as 'sharp' sand, the particles being very angular due to their granite origins. Because of this the sand was not very suitable for building purposes and was mainly used for road construction by the local Councils, and also the horticultural trade. Just before the Second World War both vessels were replaced by an iron-built, *Effort II*, constructed at Noss. She was unloaded by a steam grab which used to trundle its way up and down that short length of line along the quayside. The Langmead family of Galmpton and Torquay were associated with the extraction of river-bed sand from the latter part of the nineteenth century until 1969 when the landing of sand at both Galmpton and Totnes ceased.

*Cliff Cottage, overlooking the ebb and flow of human activity in Galmpton Creek.*

As already mentioned, another industry associated with Galmpton was quarrying. For centuries it had been the centre of quarrying for Devonian limestone within the Dart estuary. Thick beds of this rock extend from Berry Head, above Brixham, to the north and east of the area adjacent to the estuary at

Galmpton Creek. This made the creek an ideal spot for taking out the stone, together with a major by-product, lime. The estuary is dotted with many limekilns, some situated here by the quarries, and others at landing places closer to its final destination where the limestone was burnt in preparation for its use on the soil as lime.

With the estuary acting as a great highway and cargoes to be moved, there was great consideration given during the early nineteenth century to cutting a canal from Galmpton Creek through to the sheltered waters of Torbay at Broadsands in order to give greater accessibility during rough weather. Financial constraints ruled the day and any ideas of a canal were shelved.

*Mooring post and the old quarry dock at Galmpton Creek before the incoming tide of change.*

Depending on the state of the tide, make your way across the head of the creek, either across the small beach or by the roadway leading to Perrett's Boatyard. Half buried within the mud you will notice the skeletal remains of old wooden vessels, one being *Effort*, her working days of carrying sand now long gone. This second boatyard was started by Stanley Burnard Hall, mariner in 1862, one of a family much associated with Galmpton, past and present, landowners, farmers and seafarers, exemplifying the many facets of Galmpton's character. In turn, known as Dolphin Yard, Torbay Boat Construction and today, Perretts, the last boat built here in 1957 was a steel trawler *Sweet Water* working out of Brixham. Depending on the time of year you will notice an old weathered hull lying off the quay accompanied in the winter months by two better kept relations, the *Western Ladies*, who spend their summers traversing Torbay loaded down with happy holidaymakers enjoying a brief life on the ocean wave. These graceful vessels all started their lives back in the Royal Navy of the 1940s as Fairmile B Motor Launches (or MLs) and many of their sisters were built here within the yards of Galmpton Creek.

*Sunset over Galmpton Creek.*

*Canada geese gather at low tide on the mud flats at Galmpton Mill Creek.*

Considering the human activity within the creek wildlife is here in abundance. Throughout much of the year, squadrons of Brent Geese frequent the waters and mud of neighbouring creeks and their bantering calls are unmistakable as they take to the wing in their V-formations. During the quieter moments of the day, especially at dawn and sunset, the sharper cry of the oyster catchers pierce the air, whilst the silent heron and, more recently, white egrets, wait patiently in the shallows on their stilted legs.

Our route climbs steeply up the path on the southern side of the creek from where you look down on Cliff Cottage, built as the Victorian residence of Stanley Hall and originally named Rock Cottage. Over the years it has gathered a wealth of legend associated with regal hospitality and other mysteries, but its site overlooking the creek make it an enviable place of residence.

The path joins Mill Lane at a 'dog-leg' where you will find a convenient gate on which to lean while you gaze out over the Broad Reach of the estuary and its distant channel proceeding northwards towards Totnes. On the far bank of the creek lies the Waddeton Estate, often referred to locally as Watton. From this point the house is hidden by woodland but will become more visible as your walk progresses. One point of reference that is visible however, is Waddeton boathouse, shrouded in woodland that dips right down to the water's edge. The adjacent woodland is known as Tors Wood and was given, together with fishing rights, to the Canons of Torre Abbey in the thirteenth century by Lady Isabella de Wadetone as dues for the eternal safeguarding of her diseased husband's soul. Never one to waste an asset, the Canons created an ingenious salmon trap using the nearby side creek. The loose stone barrier associated with that early trap still survives.

Above: *Tors Wood and the remains of its associated medieval salmon trap.*

Left: *Waddeton Boathouse sitting snugly at the water's edge.*

Below: *Galmpton Mill ideally situated at the head of its creek.*

Now walk on down Mill Lane and on around the beach at the head of Galmpton Mill Creek. There has been a mill on this site since Tudor times, with additions being made to the structure over the centuries. You will cross the little stream that once powered the mill wheel. It was during the Napoleonic Wars that the local water mills, such as this, could not cope with the increase in demand for flour and a ring of windmills was constructed around Torbay, including one nearby at Galmpton Warborough.

Hopefully your short walk around Galmpton Mill Creek will be accompanied by the sound and sight of a variety of estuary birds as this is a reclusive and popular gathering place for terns as well as the other residents of the estuary.

You will exit the beach under the spreading boughs of an oak, but before you do have a good look at what is one of the best examples of a limekiln on the estuary. Looking across the creek you can see the quarry from where its raw material came, brought across by barge. Today this quarry is part of a boat park run by MDL. The limestone was placed in alternating layers with originally charcoal, then later culm or coal, in an inverted bell-shaped chamber, now out of sight behind the small throat visible at the base of the kiln. The 'burning' of the limestone over many hours in a restricted air supply converted it into quick-lime, a highly corrosive powder which became immensely popular from the early eighteenth century for sweetening the soil and increasing its fertility. Because of its corrosive qualities it was also used to sterilize dairies and kitchens. When water was added it became slaked lime and provided further products such as lime mortar for building and lime wash for painting. Looking at the impassive walls of weathered limestone today a realisation of its versatility highlights the economic and practical value it gave to the local community. Limestone, often referred to locally as crack-stone, was used widely as a building material and also, over the ages, as a form of ballast in ships leaving from the Dart for foreign parts. It is said that Galmpton stone was used as ballast in the ships bound for Newfoundland in the days of Raleigh and Gilbert. On arrival the stone was not wasted but was used in the building of harbour walls, shelters and fish stores.

Now climb the stile and make your way up over two fields towards Lower Greenway Farm. You are now once more on National Trust land, this being part of the Greenway Estate. You have also left the alkaline limestone area of Galmpton and have passed on to the acidic soils of Greenway where spreading lime had such a positive effect in the past. It is worth considering as you climb the hill that without Richard Harvey's intervention in the 1860s you would be crossing the route of the proposed Dartmouth & Torbay Railway!

Lower Greenway Farm comprises 240 acres. The farmhouse must be one of the most beautifully situated farmhouses in Devon, overlooking the estuary. It was built during the stewardship of Edward Carlyon, prior to 1851. The farm buildings were built as an entity, slightly later, by Richard Harvey. Their massive construction and size confirms the importance and productivity of what was a typical Devonian mixed farm of the Victorian to pre-Second World War period. Richard Harvey's investment in his farms is noticeable through the quality of the buildings and the fact that he installed a steam engine to provide power for a variety of purposes. The tall chimney associated with that engine still exists.

From Lower Greenway you have a choice of routes to take. Since the National Trust have taken over the estate a new network of footpaths and bridleways has been introduced. Keeping right, having passed through the farm buildings, will set you en route to Greenway Garden via the Greenway ferry road. Another choice is to strike left, over a stile and field, to cross the Greenway Road and then on up through Down Copse introducing you to this new network of footpaths. Keeping right and climbing up through the copse you will come out on to open pasture, finally joining the path junction on the apex of the Greenway ridge, first referred to in Chapter 7. In the past much of this land had been utilised as rabbit warrens and parkland before being returned to farmland.

*A view of Galmpton Creek from a position on the new network of footpaths within the Greenway estate, created by the National Trust.*

From here your route is left, down to the old Galmpton–Greenway trackway, with those idyllic views of distant Dartmouth, then left, back to Maypool and Higher Greenway. At Higher Greenway, having turned right, off the road, bear left up the track and not along the Dart Trail. This track, part of the prehistoric route between Brixham and Greenway, leads you up to a final breathtaking view of estuary and Torbay with distant Dartmoor visible on a good day. Following the track becoming enclosed between hedgerows, keep an eye out for a junction and turn left into what is known as Coombe Lane, albeit a green lane in character and a perfect environment for wildflowers. This beautiful ancient highway will guide you back down to the railway on the outskirts of Galmpton village and from there it is but a short walk back to the Manor Inn or the Post Office, and your circumnavigation of the Manor of Galmpton with Greenway is complete.

*Higher Greenway – a favourite spot to pause and be thankful for one's senses. An ever-changing rural scene of estuary and distant moor.*

CHAPTER 9

# *Dittisham Revisited*

The time has come to stand back and study the estuary from afar, to follow in the footsteps of ancient peoples and the rural folk who worked the soil and shaped the landscape that so many of us treasure today. Our route will start and finish in the highly sought-after village of Dittisham, escaping with an incursion into the utter peacefulness of the hills and combes of the South Hams and the pinnacle of Little Capton, nearly 600 feet (180m) above the estuary.

Dittisham provides you with excellent car parking at the Ham car park (SX865552), adjacent to the waterfront from where this walk commences. This is very much a fragmented village which adds to its charm and individuality. Its position on the western slopes of the estuary has been determined by its two-mile shoreline and the headland of Gurrow Point dividing higher from lower Dittisham. Your walk along the Dart Valley Trail in Chapter 7 introduced you to the lower village and now we will complete the picture.

Follow the access road, Ham Lane, out of the car park and up the hill. To your left an open area of meadow rises gently up the hillside providing a rural and restful break between the two parts of the village. This is known as Shinners Meadow and also provides recreational space for the local community. Be sure to enjoy the latest addition to the immediate locality, on your right – a piece of aesthetically pleasing sculptural art – 'Millennium Birds' by Bridget McCrum.

*'Millennium Birds' by Bridget McCrum.*

Ham Lane leads into Riverside Road and thence up to the centre of higher Dittisham and the Church of St George, the hub of the old Saxon village from whence it gained its name. The church, extensively fourteenth century, is

Above: *The Church of St George.*

Right: *The communal heart of the village overlooking the estuary.*

constructed of local dressed slate. Its strategic position at the centre of the community also provided a place of refuge and a lookout from its tower; present-day views of the river emphasise this point. St George's stands close by the other communal buildings of the village, the village hall (once the school), a compact post office and shop, and the Red Lion inn.

Dittisham's close-knit ties with the land and salmon fishing are all but gone, however, ironically, it is our nostalgia for the romantic idyll with this past that drives us to preserve Dittisham as it is. We will leave one last vision of Dittisham's rural bliss, where the villagers, farm labourers and fishermen once lived, for your return and now make tracks out of the village along Higher Street and the Cornworthy road.

It is a brief walk along the road before you turn up a short track to your left and enter open country through a kissing-gate. Now a right-of-way will take you up over the fields with expansive views over the South Hams countryside. Initially you will see Dittisham Mill Creek below with views of the main river channel over Blackness Point towards Stoke Gabriel. In a line directly ahead of Mill Creek over Pighole Point on the eastern side of the estuary, you

Above: *A natural framing of Dittisham Mill Creek.*

Left: *The various residences of Sandridge visible over Dittisham Mill Creek.*

will be able to identify the white pile of Sandridge. Situated between Stoke Gabriel and Waddeton, the present house, being on the left of the three structures visible, was built in 1805 by John Nash for the recently widowed Lady Ashburton. To its right you can identify what was the separate coach house and then right again, overlooking a curving indentation of the river bank set between Sandridge Point and Ladies Quay, over a gently sloping meadow, Sandridge Barton. Today the Barton's elegant Georgian façade masks the simpler Tudor structure that once preceded it. It was here that in 1543 a farmer's son, John Davis, was born, a son of the Dart and Devon who was to become one of England's greatest navigators and explorers. Of high innate intellect it wasn't long before his abilities in mathematics and an ease of learning a variety of languages brought him to the attention of the Gilberts, especially Adrian, with whom he developed a lifelong friendship. The sea provided an early draw and his marriage to Faith Fulford of Bozomzeal completed his closely entwined relationship with the influences of the Dart estuary and visions of exploration.

At the age of 42, two years after Sir Humphrey Gilbert's taking of Newfoundland and subsequent death, John Davis started on a series of expeditions to try and find the North West Passage to Cathay (China). Sailing in two relatively small craft from Dartmouth, the *Sunshine* (50 tons) and the *Moonshine* (35 tons), he explored the coastal waters between Labrador and Greenland, gradually pushing north and west. Eventually a wall of ice obstructed any further progress, but his meticulous charting of channels and currents along the north-eastern seaboard of the American continent was to provide invaluable information and accurate charts for future generations of British seafarers. The Davis Straits remain as a reminder of the skill and determination of a man so suited to his task.

The year 1588 saw John Davis' explorations curtailed in order to assist in the defence of his country whilst under threat from the Spanish Armada. A Muster of Mariners drawn up in 1570 illustrates well the number of qualified seafarers from the towns and villages of the Dart, many of whom would have joined with John Davis at this time: From Dartmouth, 28; from Kingswear, 35; from Galmpton,5; from Dittisham, 29. In total Devon registered 1250 mariners.

With the Spanish threat dissipated by English sea-dogs, fire and tempest, John Davis turned his attentions south and joined an ill-fated expedition to the East Indies via the Straits of Magellan in 1591. Being fortunate to survive he returned and at least was able to inform the queen of the discovery of the Falklands. Failure was followed by a successful privateering partnership with Sir Walter Raleigh concluding with a £20 000 cargo, including peppers and ivory being landed at Dartmouth. When not at sea, he continued to reside at Sandridge from where he wrote and published works associated with his navigational expertise, including the invention of navigational instruments such as the quadrant and backstaff.

*On the approaches to Kingston woodland and meadow characterise an ageless Devon landscape.*

In 1601 John Davis utilised his skills in a change of direction – to the East and what, from embryonic beginnings, was to become Britain's association with the Indian subcontinent. He was given the responsibility of pilot to the first convoy of the English East India Company, sailing from London in five ships, calling in at Dartmouth before leaving home waters. It was the Far East and his insatiable desire for exploration that drove John Davis to his fateful meeting and death at the hands of Japanese pirates at the age of 62, far distant from the tranquil waters of his beloved Dart.

Now turn your back to the river and follow the right-of-way over the fields to Kingston. The route is not always clearly defined and close attention will need to be taken of a 1:25,000 OS map to help you find a number of stiles along your way. However, the challenge is worthwhile in order to cross the deep valley and make the climb to Kingston, with lovely views of verdant pasture and brakes of timber, an ageless rural vista indeed.

The route now takes you through Kingston Farm, again another farming hamlet of Saxon origin and name. Most of your climbing is now done as you follow farm track and hedgerow to the hamlet of Capton, some 600 feet above the river and situated at the crown of a series of valleys which feed into the Dart. Amazingly, Capton comprised a nucleus of five farmhouses and their associated barns and linhays, with their land radiating out from the village hub. Today none of these dwellings survive as working farms, Studdy's Farm becoming a private residence in the late 1970s, but the feel for the village roots within the surrounding landscape pervades the area. The prehistoric route and ridgeway from Dittisham to Halwell and Stanborough passed close by here and it is highly likely that Bronze and Iron Age farming settlements predated the feudal administration of their Saxon successors. In late Victorian times this close-knit farming community seems to have identified strongly with the Methodist persuasion as the well-preserved structure of the Wesleyan Chapel, dated 1890, indicates. This is now a private residence.

*Studdy's Farm, Capton.*

*The soft blue of a field of flax abuts the ancient way between Kingston and Capton.*

*The shaded delights of Capton Wood.*

At the road junction just past old Chapel, turn right, down the hill, past the holiday cottages of Brown's Farm. This will lead you back out into the countryside and down along a leafy lane towards Capton Mill. One can imagine all those cartloads of grain that must have passed this way over the centuries and the straining shires hauling the sacks of flour back up the hill following a good harvest. Your route leads you off to the right, above the Mill, and then on down the side of the valley and into Capton Wood. Now managed by the Woodland Trust, its environment of dappled light diffuses the myriad uses its timber, flaura and fauna provided for the rural community in bygone days. Today it is its aesthetic values, a home for wildlife and birdlife that predominate. Following a stretch of water meadow and possibly the company of grazing cattle, you will arrive at the newly repaired Barberry Water Bridge with a chance to 'float boats' under its arch. However, you are

Right: *Barberry Water Bridge.*

Below: *The verdant mill-pool opposite Bramble Torre.*

not to cross the bridge but proceed on down the track to your right until you join the lane just above Barberry Farm. The hedgerows in this area must have been prolific in providing seasonal fruits and berries, to such an extent that local place-names have come about through association. Barberry was once a common hedgerow plant, sought for its medicinal qualities and its red berries which made an excellent jelly. The lane takes you on past Coombe and then right to the imposing four-storey mansion of Bramble Torre. On the opposite side of the road is the pleasantly situated mill-pool fed by the Capton stream that you have followed. A few yards further on and you will be accompanied, to your left, by the broad stone launder that once fed water to the wheel of Brambletorre Mill. The Capton stream, having powered two mills along its course, then finally joins the Dart at Dittisham Mill Creek.

*The now dry stone launder that once fed water to the millwheel of Brambletorre Mill.*

Dittisham Mill Creek provides two very different environments, so characteristic of all tidal creeks. High tide provides a brimful expanse of water with boats riding at their moorings. On the northern shoreline can be seen another limekiln with its little quay that once awaited its next load of limestone – from Galmpton quarry no doubt. Other Dittisham trading vessels also must have laid up in this creek, for during medieval and Tudor times, Dittisham boats participated in the salt trade with La Rochelle as well as the later Newfoundland cod trade which required large quantities of the mineral.

*A safe mooring on the thick, soft mud of Dittisham Mill Creek.*

If the tide is making (coming in), it is best you take the road in order to approach Dittisham. You will reach the point where you turned off the road into the fields on your outward leg to Kingston. Here, bear left down into an even narrower lane which will bring you into Lower Lane. However, at low tide you can take the tidal path, hugging the foreshore, with a chance to see a tidal terrain of mud flats and deep channels, a popular feeding ground for a variety of estuary birds. Steps will then bring you up off the beach into the lower reaches of Lower Lane and a chocolate-box setting of meticulously renovated cottages, once the homes of Dittisham's working community, married to the land, river or more distant seas. A gentle climb up Lower Lane will bring you back up to the Church, or the Red Lion, before you make your final descent back down to Ham Lane.

Above: *Lower Lane.*

Right: *A last look down over Dittisham Mill Creek.*

Chapter 10

# Stoke Gabriel – Salmon Village of the River

Stoke Gabriel provides yet another example of a village settlement influenced by the geography of the river. Built along the northern foreshore of a tidal creek, its original stamp of identity is Saxon, although more fragmented communities dating back to Neolithic times certainly existed hereabouts. There is no doubt that the fruits of the river, mainly in the form of salmon, were the influences behind this riverside village developing. Although Dittisham shared in this rich annual harvest, Stoke, as it is often referred to,

*Stoke Gabriel.*

has always been the centre of the salmon fishery as far as the estuary is concerned. However, unlike Dittisham, Stoke has had little association with more distant trading vessels and from that point of view has remained a relative backwater.

*William Payne's early nineteenth century painting of Stoke's tidal mills situated within the dam (or foss).*

This particular walk will provide you with a chance to explore the most attractive parts of the village, together with a considerable section of water-frontage that protrudes out into the main stream of the estuary, known as Long Stream. It will also give you an opportunity to view Stoke's little sister, the waterside hamlet of Duncannon. Your starting point is The Quay (SX847569) where there is car parking available. This is a lovely spot to linger, as many do, and it also a place from where it is possible to identify nearly every facet of Stoke's past without moving a step. The Quay is situated on the western shore of the creek and marks the point from where the dam (or foss) was built across the creek to provide a mill pool. Reminding ourselves of Dartmouth, the dam you see here today provides a living example of the ancient foss and the confined mill pool that once existed at Dartmouth back in Norman days and beyond. A sea mill, as it was called, with two wheels, was situated close to the Stoke side and was certainly still

*That same dam as seen today.*

working in 1850 when the miller was known to be Matthew Churchward. The miller's house stood cheek-by-jowl with the mill, filling a considerable area of the present quayside and café. When both dam and mill were constructed is unknown, but is likely to be of Norman origin considering the necessity for a mill and the accessibility of tidal water. The principle used was to allow the mill pool to fill with the tide using a one-way sluice-gate and then controlling the release of water through the water-wheel sluices, thus turning the drive shafts and grinding stones. Standing by the dam today at varying states of the tide provides you with some idea of the rise and fall of the river and just how distant it seems at low water. The biggest tides (Springs) give a range of 16 feet (5m) and are experienced during both Spring and Autumn.

Now, the mill pool provides a relatively static area of water and creates an ideal environment for its swans, ducks and moorhens. Water levels allowing, start your walk by proceeding along the narrow beach towards the church (use Mill Hill for access if necessary), turning into the village apple orchard through a small wooden gate. This is one of the village's few remaining orchards, once a key part of the village around which the dwellings and farmsteads were dispersed. As once the farming community produced the golden cider that was the staple drink, so today the local community protects its last orchards with determination and care, and has now brought back some of the old traditions associated with cider making. In January the ancient ceremony of wassailing is held to ward off evil spirits and encourage a good crop for the forthcoming season.

Adjacent to the orchard is the churchyard and Church of Saint Mary and Saint Gabriel. The thirteenth century church tower is the oldest part of the present building with the main body of the church being rebuilt during the fifteenth century. However, the oldest structure present is the ancient yew, situated in the churchyard. Now requiring considerable support its mighty spread is thought to date back a thousand years, to the time of the original Saxon church.

*The Church of St Mary and St Gabriel standing over the tranquil mill pool whilst its ancient yew spreads its branches ever outward to the left of the tower.*

*Church, inn and stocks provide three facets of Stoke's community in years gone by.*

From the church lych-gate runs a short cobbled street, abutted by a sympathetically constructed row of Tudor buildings and providing much of the heart of the old village. The key structure, on the corner, is the Church House Inn. It is thought to be one of the oldest 'church houses' in the county and retains its ancient cosy village atmosphere and its close affinity with the spiritual heart of the community. Close by are the old school house and the Sexton's house and, as a reminder to the transgressors of the law, the village stocks, visible for all to see.

Now take the narrow road down beside the Post Office, Coombe

Shute, passing a second hostelry, The V&A (Victoria & Albert) and then on along a narrow street of tightly-packed, but dainty terraced cottages. Where the street dips down to its lowest point, turn left up Stoke Hill and wend your way up to its junction with the Paignton Road and the site of the village War Memorial, an unusual but attractive rounded design in local limestone topped with a granite cross. Continue along the gradual incline of the Paignton Road and notice the fascinating variety of buildings and the different social strata that they would have accommodated in the past. Individual residences from Georgian to Victorian are predominant, but well balanced by the solid stone construction of Old Stoke Farm and its outbuildings, all now converted to other uses. Here again, we have another Devonshire village that was dominated by its farm, the very reason for a developing village community.

At the junction of the Paignton Road with New Road, turn left and follow along New Road with a second orchard, another protected open space, to your left. Shortly after the road curves to the left, turn right into Duncannon Lane. The lane soon leaves the confines of the village and a distant view of higher Dittisham opens up over green pastures to your left. To your right, frustratingly hidden behind a high wall, is an attractive Georgian mansion by the name of Mazonet. Rumour had it that this residence was built for one of the Prince Regent's mistresses during the early years of the nineteenth century. Along this section leave the lane and take the footpath to your left, following it over the fields and down through Duncannon Copse. Follow the path right down to the beach and Stoke Point where you can take in the curving vista of the river at Duncannon Reach, the lower section of a wonderful Z-bend and the gateway to the higher reaches of the estuary.

Looking up-river you will see the miniscule hamlet of Duncannon, situated along the water's edge. Between your observation point and the hamlet lies a quiet anchorage within a curve of the river and here it is quite likely you will see a few of the remaining salmon skiffs moored. The salmon fishery is nearly as old as the river itself and menfolk of Stoke Gabriel, Duncannon and Dittisham have been the chief players in this profession for centuries past. To conserve the salmon the rules of fishing have always been strictly adhered to by the fishermen. The season runs between 18 March and 16 August, barring Saturdays and Sundays. Back in the early 1900s there were licences for 18 boats but this has now been cut back drastically in order to try and conserve the diminishing stocks. Each boat was usually manned by a crew of three or four in the days of cotton nets. A net is cast out from the

*Salmon fishermen of the river practising an ancient skill and knowledge of the estuary, passed down from one generation to the next.*

*Duncannon.*

boat and an area of river encircled. The net is then brought to the shore and gradually hauled in. Sea Trout are also caught, especially during the early part of the season. The largest ever catch recorded was in 1921 when John Allen landed 62 salmon. In those days many salmon were sent to Billingsgate by train. If there was a shortage of ice for the journey the fish were packed in locally gathered green rushes.

The last 'professional' salmon fisherman of the river was Sidney John Collings (Sid). He made his living entirely from the river and included in his work the job of being ferryman from Duncannon across to Ashprington Point. He died in 1965, in his late eighties, having lived at Ferryman's Cottage, Duncannon since 1916. His ferry–salmon skiff was named *Eva* and he could be summoned to the Ashprington bank by the blowing of a whistle that used to hang from the branch of a tree. The ferry crossing was part of an ancient route for the people of Ashprington making their way to and from Paignton Market. Having landed at Duncannon they would wend their way up Duncannon Lane with their fully-laden baskets of produce. Another job for Sid was to respond to the whistle of a passing paddle-steamer and row out to pick up a passenger who wished to land, or, of course, to take someone out to embark.

He was indeed a busy man in the days when the river was a thoroughfare. The ferry ceased in the early 1960s. Another victim of the motor car.

Just upriver from Duncannon the shoreline is characterised by a section of tree-topped cliff. Local legend has it that this was the spot where the unfortunates and ne'er-do-wells of medieval Stoke and Duncannon were condemned to 'ordeal by water', where their chances of survival were minimal, whether guilty or innocent.

Immediately opposite Duncannon Point you will see Bow Creek disappearing into the distance. Bow Creek takes you up to Tuckenhay (see Chapter 12) and Bow Bridge and is fed by the Harbourne stream, the lowest tributary of the Dart to be fed by waters off Dartmoor. For now, however, you will turn south to make your way back towards Stoke. Should the tide be out you can walk along the shore but otherwise climb back up the steps and turn right into the field to follow a footpath that runs parallel with the shoreline. This attractive path takes you along the head of the anvil-shaped peninsula that separates Stoke from Duncannon. Every now and then you will be pleasantly surprised by a vista of distant higher Dittisham and the Long Stream of the Dart, the

Above: *Higher Dittisham visible from the western shore of Long Stream.*

Left: *Long Stream in winter.*

longest straight stretch of river channel within the estuary. Its ranks of mooring trots are crammed to capacity during the summer and ominously deserted during the season of sou'westerly gales, with recreational craft of all types and sizes safely tucked up in the various boatyards of the estuary, from Totnes to Dartmouth.

Our path climbs and turns above Mill Point to lead you back up past the neck of Stoke creek towards the weir, with a choice of the beach during low water or a higher path at high water. A very necessary pontoon is situated at the quay for sailing dinghies and tenders to allow access to the deep-water channel during the intermediate states of the tide. The variety of craft moored here provide a striking splash of colour against the natural hues of the river and woodland fringes. Given time and tide, make your way over the dam to the far bank, beneath South Down where you can explore a further area of river foreshore and look back at the more pleasing face of this historic village that has been so closely linked the waters of the Dart and the King of the River. But for how much longer?

Chapter 11

# The Secrets of Bow Creek and Beyond

The solitude and tranquillity of Bow Creek today belies what was once one of the most industrial creeks of the Dart estuary. This walk will provide a perfect insight into the close links of rural life with the quiet and efficient lines of communication provided by the river, specifically for the community of Tuckenhay, but also Cornworthy. It will also evidence how bulk cargoes and products could be transported deep into the heart of the South Hams along the narrow fingers of the estuary.

*The Harbourne stream enters the Dart at Bow Creek.*

This walk starts from Tuckenhay and one possibility of providing yourself with a parking facility is to start or finish with some refreshment at the Maltsters Inn. The quayside was once an immensely busy point of trade, with corn, malt and cider making up three important commodities being sent out by trading vessels loading from the quay. In addition, rope was manufactured from locally-grown hemp and Tuckenhay was the centre of trade, within Bow Creek, for fifteen limekilns of which a number are still visible. Limestone was brought upriver from Galmpton, Torbay and Plymouth for conversion and use on the fields of the surrounding area. Just up the lane towards Bow Bridge two kilns are in the process of being restored as a local heritage feature.

From the quay, make your way through the village, along the road in the direction of Cornworthy. Having passed the narrow curving bend, look out for the picturesque Old Bakehouse cottage on your left, and opposite, the Old Corn Mill. This building is unique in Tuckenhay in that it is constructed of red volcanic stone obtained from one of the nearby areas of volcanic intrusion found within the Ashprington area. The bakery was certainly well situated for its supply of local flour and the mill was still very much in use up to the

*The distinct red stone structure of Tuckenhay Corn Mill.*

*The intricate but imposing nineteenth-century Tuckenhay Paper Mill.*

Second World War, although by then mainly producing bran and other food-stuffs for animal feed.

Tuckenhay's creek, which now briefly runs parallel with the road, is fed by the River Wash, though not much more than a stream and rather an exaggerated status for this particular watercourse.

Continue on past the turning which leads over Tuckenhay Bridge and take the next left at Coronation Cross. At this point, the dominant feature of Tuckenhay's old paper mill becomes very apparent and it is possible to approach to the very walls of this imposing building that has played such an important part in the life of the local community in years gone by. A short, narrow road snakes its way up to Bridge Terrace, once terraced cottages for the mill workers, and on up to the right, behind the mill complex.

This paper mill came into existence during the 1830s, having most likely been constructed originally as a woollen mill, and was to continue in production until 1970. Much of its success was due to the fact that it produced a range of high quality paper using local vegetable raw materials and a plentiful supply of clean, pure water. Products included vellum parchments for deeds, bonded paper and currency notes for a number of the countries, with considerable quantities being hand-made. Later rag pulp became the main ingredient in paper production but quality remained the all-important benchmark. In 1889 the mill was considerably extended, including the building of the clock tower. It just happened that at that time St Mary's Church, Totnes was replacing its Brockeden clock and so a Mr Symons, then owner of the mill, purchased the timepiece for installation in his new tower. There the clock remains to this day. In its heyday the paper mill employed over sixty workers and of course the main method of transporting the finished product on the initial stages of its journey to distant destinations, was by river. Fortunately for all concerned, the building today, no longer required for an industrial purpose, has been beautifully restored and is used as a holiday complex.

From the rear of the mill complex it is possible to walk on up the track to join the Cornworthy road at Edgecombe Barn. From the track, or from the road on the far side of the valley, you are provided with glimpses of the leat and mill pool that provided the paper mill with its driving power and pure, clean water. However, for your recommended route, retrace your steps briefly and walk up behind the mill-workers' cottages to begin the steep climb up over, aptly named, Corkscrew Hill. Here you experience an ancient Devonshire sunken track, gouged into the hillside, the red soils richly covered in foliage and fern. As the track curves around the breast of the hill occasional gateways provide vistas of the country-side 300 feet above the river. Eventually the track leads you into the upper reaches of Cornworthy village close by Court Prior Farm on Abbey Road. Here it is worth another small diversion of a hundred yards or so to your right, to view the remaining ruins of nearby Cornworthy Priory.

*The stark remains of Cornworthy Priory's thirteenth-century gatehouse.*

All that remains today is the gatehouse of what was the thirteenth-century Augustinian Priory dedicated to St Mary. Founded by a member of the Braose family, Lords of the Manor of Totnes, it became the home of a small number of nuns, varying between 7 and 12 in number. They were mainly the unmarried or widowed daughters of local families of means and at one time included in their number Mary Pomeroy of nearby Berry Pomeroy. The Priory, although small in size (the church was only 70 feet in length) must have provided a pleasing site on the high ground above the village and the nuns were recognised for their sociability and 'worldliness' for which they were much criticised by the Bishop of Exeter!

Return down to Court Prior Farm, which must have had close association with the Priory during medieval times. The village of Cornworthy is situated on a saddle-shaped depression, high up on the hillside. Priory and parish church occupy the two opposing high points, each visible from the other. Now continue on down through the village heading towards the church. Older cottages and other dwellings associated with the rural past huddle close by farm and church with the lower lying, intervening land now more recently infilled with a bungalow development.

*The tranquil village of Cornworthy.*

Cornworthy is another village of Saxon origin, its very name providing an inkling of the past productivity of the area. It sits high above the valley and yet its lands to the north bound the foreshore of Bow Creek. As you near the church, passing the Hunters Lodge inn, the village offers a fascinating mix of architecture with local stone and thatch interspersed with simple but elegant, Georgian-style properties depicting residences of tasteful prosperity. Its tranquillity today is greatly assisted by the fact that its simple and ancient network of roads provide a natural bypass to the south of the village. The social centre of the village is marked by a noble English oak and the weathered masonry of St Peter's Church, where in the eighteenth century, John Seale of Mount Boone in Dartmouth became a regular attendant. His differences of opinion with the Holdsworths encouraged his change of ecclesiastic loyalty and he was buried here in 1777. The mounting block by the church gate draws the mind back to the times when horsepower was an essential ingredient of the rural scene, with its association of creaking leather, the warm odour of horse and the sound of clattering hooves. Close by the church was the poor house, consisting of four dwellings. With the opening of the workhouse in Totnes the buildings were converted into the village school, now the Village Hall. As with all Devon villages the community ran along the lines of self-sufficiency, or as near as was possible. Even up to the early 1900s the village possessed a post office, baker, shoemaker, two blacksmiths, and a village bobby.

To complete the next stage of this walk you do need to confirm that the tide will be suitable in order to allow you access along sections of the foreshore. Turn into the yard of Cornworthy Court Farm and follow the route down along a farm track towards the river. The descent is relatively gentle in comparison to your climb up to Cornworthy, but can be extremely muddy, during, or following, wet weather! However, the experience of being totally immersed in a rural setting is rewarding and worth muddy footwear, but be warned! The final section of the descent provides the best experience of all when a vista of Bow Creek opens before you and the waters of the estuary are once more at your feet. Downstream, to your right, you will see the confluence of Harbourne with Dart and the distant dwellings of Duncannon.

Our route, however, is to follow the foreshore upstream, back towards Tuckenhay. The right-of-way wends its way along the shoreline, rising and falling over low bluffs of hillside dipping into the muddy waters of the creek and interspersed with areas of water meadow and reed bed. It provides another perfect area for a whole variety of estuary wildlife with its tidal mud-banks receiving their twice-daily immersions and livestock from the surrounding farms browsing amongst the salt-resistant grasses with an evident liking for their brackish flavours. En route you will climb into an area that shows signs of considerable quarrying but is now well clothed in vegetation. The entire area comprises volcanic rock, being a continuation of the same igneous rocks associated with Greenway. This greenish-grey tuff, with many of the characteristics of slate, is a very hardwearing material and was used both in the building of Cornworthy Priory and also taken by river down to Dartmouth for the construction of the castles. The remains of a quay can still be found and this area became known as Tin House with the later construction of a limekiln here with a ready-made track for the carts and pannier ponies to scale the hill up to Cornworthy with their loads of lime.

*The waters of Bow Creek gently rise and fall across the shoreline meadow, whilst downstream Duncannon identifies the main stream of the Dart.*

Our path now hugs the very base of Corkscrew Hill with its narrow fringe of woodland capping the river bank. As you approach Tuckenhay, the view of the quay from a variety of vantage points can have a decidedly aesthetic feel, with light and weather conditions playing their part. You can imagine however, how the skipper of a trading vessel bringing in a cargo of stone, would have had little time to appreciate the beauty of the scene with the whims of wind and tide to concentrate on if he was not to run aground and lose both his profit and his pride.

The path turns to follow up the eastern bank of the Wash to a view across the creek to the dwellings of Tuckenhay, sitting sedately over their quiet backwater, the noise and bustle of past industrial labour now muffled by the years. A small plaque situated on the last stile you cross draws your attention to the fact that access to the Cornworthy section of the Dart Valley Trail was created and donated by Max Parrish, owner of The Old Bakehouse. Now cross Tuckenhay Bridge and it is but a short stroll back to The Maltsters.

*Tuckenhay's peaceful backwater.*

Chapter 12

# Home Reach – Totnes to Ashprington, and Sharpham

This penultimate walk brings us, very nearly, to the head of the estuary, and to the lowest bridging point of the River Dart at Totnes. We will, however, return to explore the town itself in more detail, as the subject of the final chapter. The stretches of the river associated with this walk provide the final approaches to Totnes and aptly include the relevantly named, Home Reach. Unlike many of the explorations in past chapters, this walk is best described as a braiding of the ways and the varied 'discoveries', as you make your way along the western valley side of the Dart, from Totnes down to Ashprington, and back, provides a memorable and stimulating walk, retaining close involvement with the river throughout.

Our walk starts on the older of Totnes' bridges, being the furthest downstream of the two. There has been a bridge on this site, certainly since Roman times, the original being of timber. It was the positioning of a bridge here, near to a ford, that was to lead to Totnes' developing prominence within the area. This bridge was replaced in the early thirteenth century by one of stone, which in turn was reconstructed during the fifteenth century into a seven-arch bridge, similar in structure to the present Staverton Bridge. The present elegant lines of the Georgian bridge were erected in 1820, designed by Charles Fowler who was also responsible for London's Covent Garden Market. Through much of Totnes' history the river has acted as the boundary between the town of Totnes and its very separate neighbour on the opposite bank, Bridgetown, its lands owned in Norman times by the De Pomeroy family and later, the Seymours, all very much part of the Berry Pomeroy estate.

*The elegant lines of George Fowler's Georgian bridge, constructed in 1820.*

From the bridge you have an excellent view downstream. On the left bank can be seen Steamer Quay which came into being during Victorian times with the inauguration of a stream passenger service to and from Dartmouth with, initially, fierce competition between two rival companies headed by Charles Seale-Hayne and Governor Holdsworth, both of Dartmouth. Centre-stage sits the Island, now Vire Island, named in honour of Totnes' Norman twin. It was only in 1834 that the island was joined to the bridge with the construction of a wall and infilling. This was all part of work to improve the river and its access to the area between Totnes and Langham Wood Point overlooking Duncannon Reach. Much of this stretch of river channel had been adversely affected by, ironically, an industry that added considerably to the wealth of Totnes – tin! Tin streaming during medieval times brought down large quantities of sand from the moor, silt which then clogged up the river channel. As shipping became bigger in size, vessels could not make the final reaches of the estuary, until the 1834 Act of Parliament was passed and the upper reaches were dredged and a deeper channel opened up.

Above: *The site of the Island shipyard, now an idyllic woodland park.*

Right: *Vire Island, as it is called today, viewed from the nineteenth century Totnes bridge.*

During Norman and early medieval times Dartmoor was the richest source of European tin and having passed through the Stannary Town of Ashburton, its trade route to Europe was through the inland port of Totnes. Another natural commodity to be carried downriver, was slate. In 1180 over 800 000 slates, probably from the nearby Penn Recca slate quarries above Staverton, were shipped out en route for the building of Winchester Castle. However, it was the cloth trade that provided Totnes with its greatest continuity of wealth. Up to the sixteenth century the town was consistently more prosperous than Dartmouth and ranked 15th within all the towns of England at this time. From the bridge the backs of the warehouses facing on to the river, now tastefully converted, make a fitting tribute to the town's importance as a centre of trade.

Walk down from the bridge and turn to your left along The Plains. This area was only reclaimed from marshland in the fifteenth century and yet most of the buildings that you see along the waterfront are nineteenth century. These warehouses were in active use up until the 1960s, handling a wide range of produce including grain, bacon, apples and cider. With the building of the railway to Plymouth in the 1850s a spur line from the main line to the quay was built in 1863. However, steam engines were forbidden on The Plains and so, from a gate situated adjacent to the junction of the bridge with The Plains, shire horses were then employed pulling the wagons to and from the quay. An interesting oddity within the ranks of warehouses is a beautifully renovated Methodist Chapel of Victorian origin. It remained in use until 1901 when, ironically, and I would presume, much to the horror of it previous tenants, it became a cider store!

Above: *Tastefully renovated warehouses overlooking the river channel.*

Left: *Viewed from Little Totnes, timber provides the last symbol of a trading port that spanned a thousand years.*

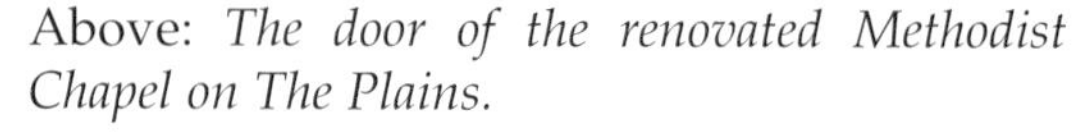

Above: *The door of the renovated Methodist Chapel on The Plains.*

Above right: *The final approach to Totnes, Home Reach, with ships unloading their cargoes of timber atBaltic Wharf, now a distant memory.*

Continue on along the line of converted warehouses into New Walk, passing the aptly named Apple House and Malt House, still in possession of its characteristic roof. A short pathway then leads you on to the quayside, once known as Town Quay, with a 180 degree view of the river and Vire Island. The quays, dwellings and workshops of this surrounding area were once known as Little Totnes, and provided the site of the earliest trading infrastructure, including St Peter's Quay, where it is highly likely all those slates were loaded back in 1180. A number of small shipyards were also associated with Little Totnes, including The Island Yard. Vessels up to 150 tons were constructed here during Victorian times. The last use of the St Peter's Quay area was for the landing and screening of river sand, only recently terminated. Very close to the quay are the visible remains of a pair of limekilns, with again the river providing ease of access for their bulky raw material. For Totnes, considerable quantities of quick-lime were required for the cleansing of sheepskins in the local woollen mills. Well situated to provide refreshment for the many local workers, including thirsty kiln workers, and those taking passage on the early river boats, was the Steam Packet Inn, still in business today but for a very different clientele.

At this point in the route you need to decide which one of two paths you are to take, either providing you with the same final destination, the alternative recommended for your return to Totnes. For the purposes of this chapter, and my personal preference, you need to take the short climb to your right, away from the Steam Packet and commence the newly inaugurated cycle path to Ashprington. Within a relatively few yards the right of way joins the route of the old Sharpham Drive and so you continue a gentle ascent of the valley side along this subtle piece of Regency engineering. As you climb you are provided with an excellent view of Home Reach and Baltic Wharf, which will be referred to on the return leg of the walk. Sharpham Drive's gentle curves lead you through a majestic rural setting of open meadow and timber brakes with the river ever-present below. As you approach Linhay Plantation the Drive reaches a height of 160 feet (50m) above the river before beginning its gradual descent to river level and the boundary of a substantial area of wetland and saltmarsh. In Regency times a stone embankment was constructed to contain the seamarsh and delineate a navigable passage along this stretch of the river. Over recent years sections of the wall have collapsed and there is a serious threat of nature and the river redefining its course. In the past, the reed beds were well utilised for basket-making as well as other commodities. Today, they provide a perfect habitat for reed and sedge warblers as well as their larger cousins, shellduck and mallards.

Above: *An attractive original nameplate attached to a gatepost en route to Sharpham.*

Left: *Saltmarsh and reed beds as viewed from Sharpham Drive.*

Above: *A stile provides access into Lower Gribble Plantation having climbed up from Sharpham Drive.*

Right: *A modern day workhorse of the river follows the tide down to Dartmouth.*

When adjacent to the saltmarsh the Drive passes through a double set of gates. Continue on along the Drive, the cycle path branching off to your right, to be used on the return leg. Soon the moment will come to leave Sharpham Drive as a waymark will direct you on to a footpath to your right, uphill across a field and into Lower Gribble Plantation. Here, joining an old track, now part of the cycle path, bear left up through the woods. The majority of the trees in this woodland are larch, one of the few deciduous conifers found in Britain, with a wonderful brake of beech providing cover along the line of the track.

At the top of the track and its junction with the lane, you will find the modern entrance to the Sharpham Estate, marked by a set of ornate pillars. Sharpham House remains a private residence but its associated vineyard is open to the public from Easter to September and is accessible down the Drive. This approach will provide you with probably the most breathtaking view there is of the upper reaches of the estuary, from Fleet Mill Reach, right up to the town of Totnes and the Church tower of St Mary's with the distant hills of Dartmoor as a very suitable backcloth. If you are able to visit the vineyard this will give you an opportunity to glimpse the house itself.

*From the higher (and modern) Sharpham Drive there are superb views of the upper reaches of the estuary, Totnes and distant Dartmoor.*

Sharpham is similar to Greenway in respect of its ideal positioning, situated high up on a promontory of igneous rock, with the meanderings of the estuary on three sides. As with Greenway the present Regency house replaced an original Tudor mansion. However, for Sharpham, the means for building this stately pile came from success in battle. Its original owner was a Lieutenant Philemon Pownoll RN and it was his share of prize money from the capture of a Spanish treasure ship in 1762 that provided the finances. Designed by Sir Robert Taylor, the conversion began in 1770 but sadly Pownoll died at sea before its completion and its first occupant was to be his daughter, Jane, as wife to Edmund Bastard. A quite substantial quay was built on the southern shoreline of the estate where Portland Stone was landed for the new construction.

Sharpham today has become well known for its wine production, its acidic soils and maritime climate proving ideal for producing high-quality grapes, another factor in common with Queen Victoria's Rhine. A walk around the vineyard will allow you to view the entire semi-circular section of the river identified as Fleet Mill Reach and Sharpham Reach with The Gut bank set between the two. From the north-facing slopes of the vineyard you can look across at Fleet Mill Quay. This now tranquil and deserted place was once

Above and right: *Regency Sharpham House with its present-day vineyard dominating the promontory below.*

quite a hive of activity for a variety of purposes. In Norman times it is thought it became a landing place for the De Pomeroys, en route to their estate of Berry Pomeroy, together with a trade route to and from the village. Then the mill itself, during its long existence at the head of its little creek, utilised river access for the transportation of its produce to Totnes and other markets. During the period prior to the 1834 River Improvement Act when the higher reaches of the river were inaccessible to larger vessels, it was here, off Fleet Mill, that cargoes were transferred into smaller craft for the final leg of the journey up to Totnes. A sign of the presence of labour required for that transfer was found in numerous clay 'baccy' pipes littering the riverbed, dropped overboard one presumes, their owners having taken a break from their labours. Lying alongside the Quay today are the remains of the penultimate *Kingswear Castle*, one of the old paddle steamers that worked the river between Totnes and Dartmouth. Taken out of service during the First World War, she was converted into a quarantine hospital ship and based at Dartmouth. Her final work done, she was towed up to Fleet Mill and there burnt out as a safety precaution and now provides excellent accommodation for river wildlife.

*The remains of the paddle-steamer* Kingswear Castle *lie against the bank at Fleet Mill Quay.*

*A Jersey heifer, one of the herd at Sharpham who provide the raw material for the estate's other prized product, Sharpham cheese.*

From the Drive entrance of Sharpham continue on along the lane into Ashprington, a village with many close ties to Sharpham. This village is another of the Dart's peaceful backwaters and is characterised by the uniformity of its neat stone estate cottages positioned around the war memorial and overlooked by the weathered form of the fourteenth century Church of St David. Much of the present look of the village was due to Richard Durant, Master of Sharpham and Squire hereabouts, who modernised the buildings and built the village school around 1847. He was obviously a man who had a strict sense of self-discipline for both himself and his tenants. He laid down a levy of fines for swearing in public places ranging from one shilling for a labourer to five shillings for a gentleman! Should you feel really energetic or prefer to return at a later date, a walk down the lane from the village to Ashprington Point, overlooking Duncannon, can be a very enjoyable experience with a further sample of differing views over the estuary, especially the lake-like expanse of Long Stream or little Bow Creek. Take a moment to reflect on those days before our reliance on the motor car when for the inhabitants of Ashprington this was the weekly trudge down to the Duncannon Ferry and on to Paignton market with baskets of produce – whatever the weather.

*The Church of St David, Ashprington.*

*Glimpses of the estuary through the larches of Lower Gribble Plantation.*

For the return to Totnes, retrace your steps, past the entrance to Sharpham and down through Lower Gribble Plantation. Here though, remain on the cycle path, which will bring you back down to the pair of gates at the head of the saltmarsh. Having passed through the gates turn off Sharpham Drive along a grassy footpath to your right and follow the hedgerow along the edge of the field. This path then becomes well-defined as it follows the edge of the saltmarsh along the edge of a low bluff. From a number of vantage points you will gain a good view across the river at a small group of ruined buildings situated on the 300 foot skyline. This was once known as Windwhistle Cottage with its associated barn. It was such an exposed spot that the cottage was constructed without any windows in its north-facing wall. The last occupants of this exposed dwelling were the Steer family, with a brood of nineteen children! Mr Steer worked on a neighbouring farm and was also known locally for his veterinary skills. Local legend has it that when coal was off-loaded from a boat for delivery to Windwhistle Cottage the men would race each other up the hill with their loaded barrows!

The variety and setting of this low riverside path oscillate from stretches of open meadow to small woodland brakes shading the river bank through which the path burrows its way. The experience is completed by a small, disused quarry area, now transformed by a luxuriant growth of fauna and lichens into a mysterious grotto within which is set the ruinous remains of a worker's cottage.

*The exposed ruins of Windwhistle Cottage.*

Eventually you will emerge out into the open view of Totnes whilst between path and river are the varied buildings and quayside of Baltic Wharf. This top stretch of Home Reach is as straight as a die as its course is constricted between wharf and Longmarsh. As its name indicates, Longmarsh was once just that, but then in Victorian times a considerable section was drained and filled to become a rifle-range for the Totnes Volunteers. Today it has become an area of accessible open parkland providing an excellent stroll along much of Home Reach. However, its south-easterly tip has been conserved as an area of special wetland interest supporting flora and fauna that is amenable to a combination of fresh and salt water. Baltic Wharf came into being in 1895 when sailing schooners brought in cargoes of timber on the high tide. The source of the majority of this softwood timber was the Baltic countries and this trade was managed by a well-known local family by the name of F.J. Reeves. Their name and timber importation through Totnes continued for the best part of a century with Baltic Wharf immersed under loads of timber and the sound of spinning saw-blades reverberating within the valley.

For something like a thousand years the tides of the estuary have been worked by commercial craft. During September 1993 Dave Griffiths, the Dart's last river pilot, tied M.V. *Conto* alongside Baltic Wharf with the last cargo of timber. Totnes is no longer a commercial port but, in keeping with the times, today the wharf is associated with recreational craft of all shapes and sizes.

It is very much in keeping with the maritime history of the river and in the adventurous spirit of the Raleigh-Gilberts that Pete Goss constructed his technically challenging *Team Phillips* in the most southerly of Baltic Wharf's sheds. This adventure was to end in failure, as did those of many of our Tudor predecessors but without the initial challenge, success is impossible and, after all, Virginia is now a part of the most powerful country in the World!

*Team Phillips en route to Dartmouth and an unforgiving sea.*

Chapter 13

# The Town of Totnes

To be provided with one town of interest and character, such as Dartmouth, is an asset. To be endowed with the benefits and charms of two, is beyond measure, and yet this is the case as far as the Dart estuary is concerned. Totnes, lying at the head of the estuary, provides a counterbalance to its sister at the mouth but as a unique gem of the estuary, in its own right. Totnes today exudes history and heritage and yet provides a vibrant community of all generations. A planned walk to explore the town's past is not envisaged for

*The lowest bridging point of the Dart, bringing together the communities of Totnes and Bridgetown.*

this chapter, but more in keeping with its compactness and intimacy, a sampling of events and edifices that have added to the story of Totnes. From this it is hoped you will be inspired to just wander and delve deeper into the many charms of this fascinating town.

As with all the communities of the estuary, Totnes owes its existence to the river and, rather like Dartmouth, has grown out of its very waters. Legend tells us how Brutus the Trojan sailed up the Dart in pre-Roman times and casting out a granite boulder on to the shore, identified the site of where a new trading port should come into being. The Brutus Stone in Fore Street marks that mythical spot. Indeed, in prehistoric times the tidal river encroached over much of what is Totnes today in the form of inlet and saltwater marsh. Standing out into this considerable area of wetland ran a ridge, or nose, of land, similar but of less height than that of Hardness at Dartmouth. The word Tot identified a 'lookout' to the Saxons and hence their creation of a settlement here – Totness!

Below: *East Gate, a fine gateway to a prestigious town.*

Situated at the head of the navigable river and at the lowest crossing place the site was of great strategic importance. As such it became one of King Alfred's defensive burghs in conjunction with Lydford, Exeter and Barnstaple, all developed as strongholds to combat Viking incursions. The demarcation of the original Saxon town, enclosed by a defensive earthen bank, topped with a timber palisade, is easily recognised today through the later medieval wall, its surrounding streets and town gates. The importance of the town was then reflected in its status as a mint town, providing coinage for the local economy and also replacing Stanborough as the administrative hub of the area. A thousand years ago, therefore, Totnes was an important trading port, more than likely involved in the movement of Dartmoor tin. At this time Dartmouth did not even exist, only the small settlement of Tunstal at the top of the hill representing the future town.

Norman influence and domination of Totnes remains squat and obvious 900 years after their arrival in the form of Totnes Castle. Following William the Conqueror's successful subjugation of the Westcountry Totnes, together with a further hundred manors, was given to Judhael the Breton and it was he who stamped his authority on the town with the building of the castle. Today it remains the best example of a Norman motte (mound) and bailey (courtyard) castle in Devon. To provide the site Judhael had to demolish eighty Saxon houses but then this must have added to the sense of subjugation and a view from the ramparts of the keep confirms the total domination that this building had over both town and river.

Left: *The Norman castle of Totnes, built to subjugate the populace below its walls.*

Below: *Norman keep and the church of St Mary, two dominant landmarks.*

Once secure, Judhael then turned his attention to spiritual matters with no doubt an eye to the future of his soul. He founded and endowed a priory as a cell of St. Nicholas' Abbey at Angers on the Loire. It was situated within the north-eastern sector of the town, within the present churchyard of St. Mary's. The Church of St Mary was rebuilt in its present form during the 15th century, adjacent to the priory and very much reflecting the opulence of Totnes' merchant class. Once again the river played its part in bringing in both Paignton red sandstone for the main body of the church and Beer stone for the making of, amongst other structures, the intricate rood-screen. With the Reformation and Dissolution of the Monasteries, Totnes Priory was mainly demolished but at the disposition of Edward VI in 1553 the refectory was converted for the multi-purpose use as guildhall, school and prison! A variety of routes will take you to this fascinating and attractive building, one being along the Ramparts Walk from the East Gate. The octagonal granite piers used to support the front of the present building were added in 1897 having been utilized from the demolition of the Fruit Market House that once stood to the south of the church.

*Totnes Guildhall, situated on the line of the town wall and once providing the additional services of Grammar School and prison!*

During the sixteenth and seventeenth centuries the town was largely rebuilt by its successful merchants and took on the architectural character so recognisable and highly treasured today. The merchant houses and shops along either side of High Street continued to spill outside the town walls and descend along the line of Fore Street towards the river. The scarcity of space largely compacted individual properties to one room in width and therefore they expanded to the rear, often including a small courtyard or garden within their boundaries. The Museum, in Fore Street, provides just such a perfect example of a typical Elizabethan merchant's house.

The heart of the town remained within the walls and close to the church where the various market commodities were sold on either side of the High Street. Today, the covered ways of the The Butterwalk and opposite, Poultry Walk, continue to provide their shade to passers by, whilst the open market area once held the Flesh Shambles. The entire locale reflects the intricate individuality of timber-framed house fronts, interspersed with areas of slate-shingle in hues of blue and grey, ideal for keeping out the Devon weather.

From the broader market area of High Street the thoroughfare tapers into The Narrows and wends its way towards the site of the town's western gate. Close by you will find the Kingsbridge Arms, situated on the old road out of Totnes. From here it is but a short step to The Leech Wells, natural springs that were said to have medicinal properties.

Far left: *Elizabethan merchant's house in Fore Street, now the Museum.*

Left: *The Narrows.*

*The Royal Seven Stars, hostelry, coaching house and inn for generations past.*

From the modernised nineteenth-century East Gate, Fore Street leads you down to The Plains and later developments of Totnes' heritage. The Civil War saw the introduction of a decline in trade, both in cloth and tin but Totnes' popularity as an entrepot, market centre and 'residential' town gathered pace. Stylish eighteenth and nineteenth century town houses began to appear, of which The Mansion, situated on the south side of Fore Street, is a fine example. Built as a gentleman's residence c.1795 it then became the boys' Grammar School from 1887 until the 1960s. One of the Grammar School's most famous students in late Victorian times was Charles Babbage who is acknowledged as being the father of computer technology. On the very boundary of The Plains, a hostelry, The Seven Stars, was to develop and prosper, providing sustenance and accommodation for both the numerous traders attending the commercial facets of the town and the more genteel of society visiting a well thought of market town. The origins of The Seven Stars are thought to be associated with a thirteenth-century chapel situated close by the bridge. In those days a religious house was often provided with an associated hostelry for the needs of its visiting travellers and pilgrims. The sign of the seven stars illustrated that the building was dedicated to St Mary, who traditionally wore seven stars in her celestial crown. A visit to The Seven Stars today will still provide you with an insight into its heyday as a coaching house with its once busy courtyard now a centrepiece of the present hotel. Many gentlemen of status have rested here over the years, including Daniel Defoe in 1720 who remarked 'that Totnes is a very good town of some trade, but more gentlemen in it than traders of note.' During the 1790s the traveller and antiquarian, the Reverend John Swete used the inn whilst in the area. 'A very pleasant house, managed by extremely civil people and affording very good accommodations.'

He was obviously also quite taken with the cuisine and the manner of its capture. 'I had quickly a beefsteak with a fine salmon peal on the table – for which fish the place is famous, and Books tell us an odd story of their being caught by means of a dog who is instructed to swim after them in the water and drive them into the nets.' It is then also highly likely that William Turner stayed here during his two visits to the Dart in 1811 and 1814 when he sketched the area profusely. The Royal prefix to the Seven Stars was to await the arrival of Britannia and officer-cadet training at Dartmouth in 1863, as did the Royal Castle Hotel at Dartmouth. From that era onward Royal sons training at Dartmouth were to frequent the now Royal Seven Stars for on a number of occasions.

Standing proud on The Plains, opposite the Royal Seven Stars is a granite obelisk, a symbol to the spirit of Victorian adventurism and a commemoration to William Wills, born across the road at No.3, The Plains. Wills, together with Burke were to be the first Europeans to cross Australia from south to north, but tragically perished on the return journey.

*The memorial to explorer William Wills.*

From the old Totnes bridge the estuary has one final meander to make before finding its most northerly point. Within this meander was once a great area of tidal salt-water marsh, known as Town Marsh situated around the north-eastern base of the Totnes ness. This area has now been totally drained and utilised for housing and commercial use. It is apt that for the conclusion of our tour of Totnes, and the estuary as a whole, we return to the river and the source of power that it has provided to communities along its length. To the north of the Plains, adjacent to the modern Coronation Road, is the site of the old Town Mill. A pair of mills were first recorded on this site as early as 1368, one for grinding corn and another for fulling cloth. A further corn mill was situated slightly further up-stream. All three were initially tidal mills fed by a leat from a mill pool within the area of the Town Marsh. By the fifteenth century a source of fresh water was added with the construction of a weir on the Dart and diversion of an appropriate quantity of water to the mills. The industries of the eighteenth and nineteenth centuries were to continue using this water as a source of power and in their processing, with Harris' Bacon Factory being the last beneficiary of this natural resource. We are lucky today that Town Mill is under the guardianship of Totnes Town Mill Trust who have created an imaginative and detailed Interpretation Centre and a site for Tourist Information.

Whilst the Town Mill Leat takes a more direct route from its source the river estuary wends its way up along its final mile from the old Totnes bridge to

Totnes Weir. A sandy spit of land, Snipe Island, has been created by the confluence of Dart with its tributary, the River Hems, but is now dominated by the site of the intrusive but necessary Water Treatment Works. Then, having passed under the Plymouth to Exeter Railway line, the final few yards of river estuary once again regain a rural identity. The last gasps of tidal influence reaching the sloping barrier of the weir are confined to high spring tides. The broad river channel below, briefly taking on the character of a mature lady, lazily following her course across this miniscule flood plain, and, having, over the centuries, deposited her moorland river gravels and sands at the head of England's most romantic and beautiful river estuary, prepares to meet the constant heartbeat of the tidal Dart.

*The last gasp of the tide rounds a broad bend in the river to meet the fresh waters of the Dart at Totnes Weir.*